P9-CRB-748

WOMAN BETWEEN THE WIND

Heather Hughes-Calero

Cover Painting and Illustrations by
Charles Frizzell

Higher Consciousness Books
1990

WOMAN BETWEEN
THE WIND

Cover painting by Charles Frizzell
Illustrations by Terry McCarty
Cover design by Lois Stanfield

Higher Consciousness Books
Shipping and orders should be addressed to Post Office Box 1797, Cottonwood, Arizona 86326. (602) 634-7728.

Printed in the United States of America

Library of Congress Catalog No.: 89-82151
ISBN: 0-932927-07-6

Other books
by Heather Hughes-Calero

Writing as a Tool for Self-Discovery

The Golden Dream

The Sedona Trilogy
  Book 1: Through the Crystal
  Book 2: Doorway Between the Worlds
  Book 3: Land of Nome

This is a true experience; however, the names of places, persons and facts may have been altered to protect the privacy of those involved.

**With love and appreciation
to Alana**

The Shape Shift
Between the Wind

Listen!

　　　The wind calls me from my left.

I look out my window. The snow
speaks to me of stories found on the
surface of the breathing earth.

　　　The snow parts, the earth
　　　breathes, the sun shines.
　　　The trees stand naked with
　　　branches defining the wind.
　　　The wind appears speaking of energy,
　　　through visionary maps the branches
　　　define on the surface of infinity.

My heart.

　　　My quiet heart
　　　　　　returns with stories.

　　　Now – My heart beats;
　　　the wind is no longer invisible.
　　　　　My fear. My fear
　　　of her power, her sound
　　　her presence. My fear is now
　　　lessened.

She is my breath, my aloneness, my
joy, my uneasiness. She is around me.
She goes inside & outside of me.
She is everywhere.

　　　I am transcending.

I have become the current in the sky.

　　　I am between her. She is between
　　　me. Both reaching for the other side.
　　　Both kissing what we are not,
　　　Always trapped on the
　　　　　otherside.

　　　　　We fight to get out.
　　　　　We fight to get in.

We meet each other after the fight —
　　　In the calm
　　　In the land
　　　　　In between

　　　　　　　　　　　—Alana

TABLE OF CONTENTS

PROLOGUE

When I received word that I had inherited my Uncle Farley's ranch outside a small town in the Colorado wilderness, I had just finished my fifth New Age book and was wrapping up a screenplay inspired by Milarepa's famed quote: "The environment I see and relate to is a symbol of my consciousness. By taking appearances as illustrations means I know all appearances are illusionary." I had ideas about what my next book would be; that is, I knew the seed of the story, which was to show how an individual could separate thought from consciousness and thereby live in a state of total awareness, but I had not yet determined how I would set the story. It seemed there was something I needed to experience before it would flow and, although I was aware that something was needed, I didn't know what it was. An invisible wall seemed to stand between me and the story I wanted to write. I had no idea of what formed the wall or how to move beyond it. Consequently, I was restless and ready for something new, something that would spark a change in me that would lead me into the experience I needed to get my work under way. When the opportunity came to take possession of my uncle's ranch, which would mean stepping away from my ordinary environment, I sensed an appealing adventure and decided to go there for a few months.

My family and my friends tried to dissuade me. Everyone expressed concern and cautioned me about the dangers of living in a place that was so remote. It worried them that my uncle had led a mysterious life, unknown to my family and the world at large. Not even the attorney who handled his estate seemed to know much about him and the only person who contacted me was a real estate agent from the nearby town of Eastcliffe, who was interested in parceling off the land. All the same, I ventured into that world alone, bold and adventuresome, certain that I was inwardly equipped to handle whatever would come my way.

"The mastery of life stands as your ultimate goal. Mastery is bliss, though some shall attempt to convince you otherwise."

Handbook for Advanced Souls
by Mark Little

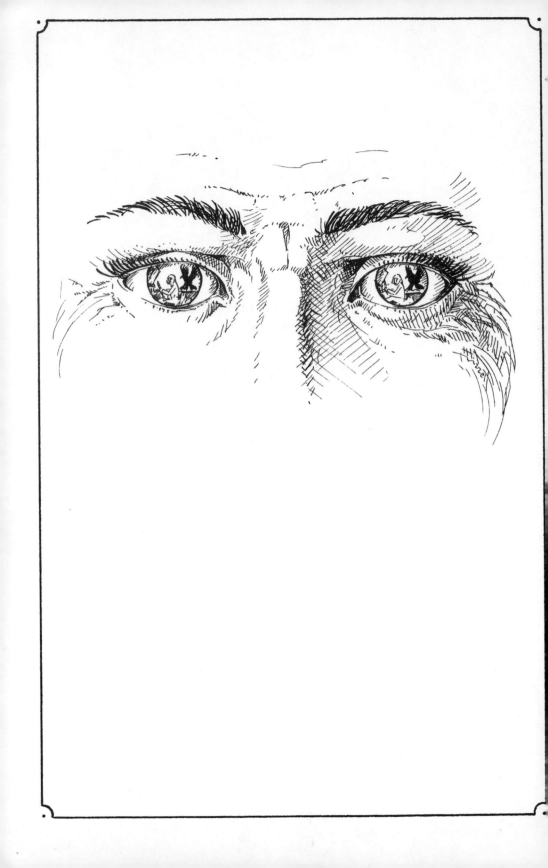

CHAPTER ONE
"INHERIT THE WIND"

With the last of the supplies loaded, I climbed into my Jeep, where I was surprised to find a middle-aged Indian woman dressed in baggy coveralls and an emerald green shirt. She grinned at me from the passenger's seat.

"It's going to be raining out at Farley's Ranch," she said.

Farley's Ranch was now my ranch. I stared at the woman, wondering what she was doing in my Jeep. At ten in the morning, it was already in the eighties, a storm was brewing and I wanted to get going. "I suppose you need a ride out that way?" I asked, trying to recall whether I had seen the woman in the grocery store.

"Don't need anything," the Indian woman answered. She eyed me from my waist up before continuing. "But you might."

I pushed open the Jeep door and started to step out, to show the woman that I wanted her to leave, but an inner nudge made me turn and look at her again. I saw that she had lowered her eyes and was fidgeting with her hands. I was sorry that I had been so abrupt.

"Look, you can ride with me as far as the turnoff," I said.

She looked up, and I realized that her age-old face was both firm and gentle. Her eyes were deep-set and luminous and, as I looked into them, I had the uneasy feeling that I could see into her, only it wasn't the Indian woman that I saw, but someone else. It occurred to me that her face was merely a mask.

"That's very kind of you," she said, "but I'm going all the way to the ranch. I live there."

"You live there," I repeated, staring at the woman.

She nodded her head. "Practically all of my life."

"My uncle's attorney said nothing about you," I said, curiously.

"I don't imagine so." The woman spoke kindly. "I don't own anything and don't need to own anything." She paused, studying me. "Some people can't come here and enjoy the land unless they own it. Seems that owning land gives them a reason to be on it. Not me. I live on it, because between the land and me, there's a kin. Do you know what kin means?"

"It means you feel a closeness with it," I answered, curious.

"More than that," the Indian woman said. "It means there's love between us. The land loves me as I love it."

"What about my uncle?" I asked, uncertain where her thoughts were headed.

"Your uncle owned the land, and he was kin to it as well," she answered. "He was also kin to me."

I studied the deep, gentle lines of the old woman's face. There was something about her that was deeply moving, although I couldn't decide what it was. "I don't know much about my uncle's life," I said finally.

She didn't seem to hear what I had said. "When you inherited the ranch, I decided to stay on," she went on to say. "It seemed to me you needed someone you can trust." She paused, looking deeply into me. "You're a writer and you have no experience at ranching. I can advise you when things come up." She paused again, glancing out the window and then back at me, rolling her shoulders in a forward motion. "Of course, until you're sure you want me, I'll stay out of the way. So will the others."

Surprised, I stared at her. "What others?" I asked.

"You don't think your uncle ran the place by himself, do you?" the Indian woman replied.

"I was told he had no livestock, just open land," I said, studying her. "Why couldn't he run it by himself?"

"He was a special man," the woman said, and then she changed the subject. "He always said you were like him and that's why he wanted you to have the place. He also said that you were smart enough to maintain your freedom so that you could give in to your need to spend time at the ranch alone."

I was surprised by the familiarity with which she spoke. It was right: I needed time alone to write and so I had arranged to set up the ranch as a retreat, where those I loved would visit me from time to time. But how did a stranger know so much about me? While I had often thought of my uncle, and even dreamed of him in my sleep, I hadn't communicated with him in years. "Who are you?" I asked.

"The name is Alana," the woman said, a sudden twinkle in her eyes. They were deep blue eyes; I was surprised by the color and wondered why I hadn't noticed it before. I had never seen an Indian with blue eyes. Then she said her name again, accenting it as Ah-lana so that the sound stuck in my mind. Her expression changed, and she looked at me in a hard, deep way for a long moment.

I looked away.

"And if you decide to have me help you, " Alana said in a quiet way, "it'll cost you, but not in money."

Her tone of voice startled me and I let go of the door handle and backed out of the Jeep, uncertain, studying the age-old face. The feeling that there was something absurdly familiar about her was unshakable. "Have we met before?" I asked.

It seemed for a moment that she was going to smile but she didn't. "It would seem that way," she answered.

I nodded soberly. "Yes, it would," I said hesitantly. I tried to focus my full attention on her, but a feeling of uneasiness made me look away. I wondered why.

"Will you take me to the ranch?" Alana asked.

I raised my eyes to meet her's and nodded again, aware that in that moment she was all I could see. The grocery store and the rest of the town were diffused and soft in outline, barely visible. "Yes Alana," I said, "I'll take you to the ranch, but I can't promise you a job." I felt that we were distant from the rest of the world, as though we were isolated together in a dream. "I need to be by myself for awhile and get settled," I added.

She smiled as if she understood.

I reached into the Jeep and gripped the steering wheel to hoist myself back into the driver's seat. "Tell me about my Uncle Farley," I said, remembering my one and only meeting with him when I was nine. I had stared up at a powerful man, hearing my mother introduce me to my Uncle Farley. He had a shaggy blonde beard, short-cropped hair and blazing blue eyes. He was totally unlike my father, who had dark hair and dark skin. "You take after your Uncle Farley," my mother had said, referring to my blonde hair and blue eyes. I remembered my mother anticipating his visit, nervous because my father resented him. My father believed my uncle had robbed him, but I never knew of what. I remembered him as a giant man with a shocking appearance who lifted me high over his head. He held me close to him for a long moment before he put me down, squeezing me as he told me that one day the finest piece of land in all of Colorado would be mine. He reached into his pocket and pulled out a shiny black stone, and handed it to me. He said it was a lodestone, and that its magnetic pull would keep the connection between his heart and mine. My reverie was interrupted by Alana's voice.

"I worked with Hugh Farley many years, just like I'm going to work with you, if you'll have me," Alana said.

I hesitated, unsure of what to say.

"I won't stay around you, unless you want me to," she added, looking directly at me.

"I really don't think I'll need any help Alana," I said, trying to be kind. "Although I appreciate the offer."

There was a long silence between us.

"I'm sorry," I added.

"There will be times that you'll be glad to have me around." Alana responded as if she had not heard me.

I hesitated, anxious to get to the ranch before the rains began.

"Not to worry," she added.

I looked at her. "I'm not worried," I answered.

"I understand you," Alana said. "Your uncle talked about you all the time."

"That's impossible," I said uneasily.

She looked at me and smiled.

"I met my uncle only once," I told her. "I never really knew him."

"He knew you," Alana said firmly. "Your uncle was some special man."

I waited for her to continue but she looked the other way, pointing to the clouds forming overhead. In a voice that was calmly authoritative, she said, "We better get going. It'll rain soon and when it rains in these parts, there'll be waterfalls to behold."

I slammed the Jeep door and started the motor. For an instant I could see my uncle's face in my imagination, and I thought to myself that he and Alana might be the source of a great story.

Eastcliffe was a little town, just a post office, two gas stations, a grocery store, a feed barn, a real estate office, and a movie theatre. We were out of it in two or three minutes and, once it was behind us, there was no traffic, nothing but open land in front of us and mountains in the distance. We drove silently, gazing at the vast terrain, upset only by an occasional rut in the poorly paved road. Although neither of us spoke, Alana's presence continued to inspire the inexplicable feeling that I had known her for a very long time. Once in a while I glanced her way, but she sat with her eyes closed, facing straight ahead. I believed her to be in deep thought rather than asleep, but I couldn't be sure. As the miles passed, my interest rose. I wondered about the Indian woman, how she had come to live at the ranch, and what it would be like if she stayed on.

As we drove, the distant mountains gradually loomed larger and larger. Some forty or fifty miles later, I pulled over to the side of the road and drew a map from my handbag. Alana opened her eyes and looked at me.

"You lost?" she asked.

I shook my head. "No, just checking."

"The ranch is at the foot of those mountains," Alana said.

I looked up from the map and hesitated, staring first at the mountains and then at her. Something about her appearance had changed, as though the years had drifted from her during the quiet drive and she was a young woman again.

"Heather," she said, turning to look at me as she spoke my name for the first time, "we had better hurry. The rain is coming."

I glanced up at the darkening sky and drove the Jeep back onto the roadway. The mountains ahead towered fourteen thousand feet above us. The land just beneath them, some 6800 acres, had been my uncle's, and it was now mine. The beauty of the area was thrilling.

"I'm glad you like it," Alana said, as though listening to my thoughts.

I moved my eyes from the road and gazed into hers, caught for a split second by my image reflected in them. Her eyes were deep and reflective. In them, I saw the Jeep, myself sitting in it and, in the background, a giant, low-flying bird, like an eagle, preparing to land. The scene was like a photograph, but reflected in her eyes, it was multi-dimensional and filled with life. Startled, I looked away.

Alana pointed ahead to a fork in the road. "Veer off to the right," she instructed. "It'll take us onto the ranch."

The road narrowed to a single lane.

"Straight ahead," Alana said.

For a long moment neither of us spoke, and my mind was completely still. Alana pointed to an eagle overhead, and broke the silence, asking, "What sort of book are you writing?"

"A very special book, I hope," I answered simply.

"I'm sure of that," Alana said.

"Do you read, Alana?" I asked, somewhat surprised.

"Yes," she said. "Tell me about your book."

I glanced at her and then returned my attention to the bumpy road. "I want to write a story about a person who learns to live from consciousness rather than thought," I said, matter-of-factly, not really expecting her to understand. "A story about someone who learns to live from the viewpoint of pure awareness, rather than the mental ramblings of thought," I elaborated, then hesitated, feeling unclear. The familiar feeling of being locked inside of myself came upon me. "Of course, we all need to think sometimes," I added stupidly.

Alana ignored my uneasiness. "What are you going to call this book?" she asked.

My fingers tightened on the steering wheel as I gazed up at the mountain range directly ahead. "I'm not sure of the title," I said. "I've been thinking of something like *Enter the Silence.*"

"Hmmm," Alana said thoughtfully, "It's a good title, but I've got a better one for you."

I was surprised. "You do?"

"Yep."

I didn't believe that she really understood the concept that I had explained so I didn't ask what she had in mind.

"When you want the title, you can ask me," she said again.

I smiled, without expectation. "Okay, what is it?" I asked.

"*B e t w e e n   t h e   W i n d,*" she said slowly, accentuating the words by spitting them between her teeth.

A slow chill traveled up the back of my neck and I accidentally swerved the Jeep into a rut on the side of the road.

Alana didn't say anything.

The long, narrow roadway twisted and turned and then straightened again. The country was beautiful, grandiose in natural expression. As we entered the mountains they seemed to become even greater, until they seemed to swallow us up, surrounding us almost completely. We were in the heart of them.

"The ranch has got both a lake and a river," Alana said, "and both are filled to the brim with drinkable water."

I turned my head, aware of a twinkle in her eye. "So I heard from the real estate office," I said, returning my attention to the road.

"What did you see them for?" Alana asked.

"They wanted me to sell the place but I told them no," I answered.

"Probably wanted to split it up into little pieces and build cardboard houses on the pieces," Alana said disgustedly.

"Probably," I agreed, not wanting to discuss it further.

"And they'd kill all the horses for dog meat, I suppose."

"What horses?"

"Didn't they also tell you about the wild horses?"

I turned and looked at her again. "No."

She let out a sigh and looked straight ahead.

"What about the horses?" I asked, looking from the road, to her, and then at the road again.

"You'll find out."

I started to question her, but ahead was a rail fence and, behind it, a stone ranch house. I recognized it from the photographs sent by my attorney, but it was prettier in real life. The house was framed by the magnificent terrain in a way which a camera could not possibly capture. The mountains and valley were awesome and enchanting.

I drove to the front of the house and brought the Jeep to a stop, gasping with delight, unable to hide my initial thrill at seeing the place. It was beautiful, not manicured beauty, but wild beauty. A carpet of golden wildflowers covered the land in all directions as far as I could see, to the feet of the towering mountains. The sky was cobalt blue, accented by an occasional milk-white, puffy cloud; there was a large rain cloud off to the right. The scene was beyond my expectations. I opened the Jeep door and got out.

"I feel like I'm dreaming," I said aloud. Slowly, I turned to look in all directions.

"Look!" Alana called.

I looked. An eagle soared overhead, and the air was filled with the sounds of smaller birds chirping. I watched the eagle disappear beyond the horizon, and then turned my attention to the small and large groves of pine and aspens that marked the landscape for miles in every direction. Standing, listening to the sounds of nature and the hush of silence within it, I heard a faint rush of wind, only I felt no wind, and I took this as a sign that I was welcome.

"Look!" Alana called again.

As though in a dream, I turned at the sound of her voice, but she was nowhere to be seen. The golden wildflowers, glistening in the early afternoon sun, grew right up to the house, touching it. I walked over to the house and ran my hand down along the rough grey stone wall, noticing the drawn window shades. The remote house appeared well cared for, and, I stepped curiously up onto the wooden porch and put a hand on the heavy wooden door. I tested the latch and found that it was locked, so I opened it with my key. When I went inside, Alana was standing in the center of the living room, in front of a massive stone fireplace, thick plank floors reflecting her presence. I hesitated, staring at her, wondering how she had gotten into the locked house.

She grinned at me. "Isn't it a wonderful place?"

I started to speak, but my attention was drawn by movement outside the house. I went to a window, drew the shade, and looked outside. It was raining, and a doe and her fawn were tiptoing past the Jeep.

When the deer had passed, I turned to Alana again, but she was gone.

For the next week, I busied myself with settling into the house and becoming acquainted with the land. I moved my uncle's desk from a bedroom to the living room window where I had seen the deer, and used it as my writing spot. In the mornings, I sat there and wrote in my diary, knowing that when I became truly acquainted with the place, the beginning of my book would come to me. Until then, I would keep track of my daily life, noting the cycles of becoming accustomed to my new world. For the most part, I wrote about the Indian woman Alana, wondering why she had left so quickly, and why she hadn't visited me at the house, and I remembered comments she had made during our Jeep ride to the ranch. Over and over again, I reflected about her feeling that she held a prominent place in my life, and her suggestion that the title of my book be "Between the Wind". Occasionally, I would say her name aloud, trying to recall the slight accent in her voice as she had pronounced it: "Ah..lana."

The life I had left in the city and the people who had been close to me now seemed far removed. My uncle's world dominated me and I viewed it as bits and pieces of him, deciding on the type of person he was by the kind of life I could now see that he had lived. I was sure that he had had a peaceful life filled with natural splendor, and that it had been exciting as well. In the solitude of his home, I found great joy in watching the wild animals, seeing how they responded to the slightest change in the environment. A cloud passing in front of the sun, causing a shadow to drape a section of the ground, could excite a deer to run as though it was being chased; a sudden gust of wind invited birds to display their acrobatic skills. And of course, there was Alana. However brief my encounter with her had been, her mysterious disappearance still highlighted my consciousness. As the days passed her invisibility became a greater mystery to me. I constantly imagined ways of drawing her into the open, but I took no action. Instead I waited, filling my diary with notes about her, writing down everything I could remember, emphasizing her most unusual qualities, such as her eyes, and her manner of speech and movement, so quietly powerful and seemingly self-contained. My notations about her bordered on the bizarre, and the more I fantasized about her, the more she became an enigma to me, unreal and many-faceted, a hundred people all rolled in one. In memory, I could still feel the great depth of her eyes as she looked into me, and I began to accept the inexplicable feeling that she was going to change the course of my life; that because she represented my uncle's reality, she was to be a central character in my book and that the story would describe my adventures with her.

As I sat gazing out the window over my desk, I wondered where Alana could be. I speculated that she must be living somewhere in the hills with the "others" she had mentioned. I tried to imagine my uncle's relationship with her, and with the others, and assumed that the others were also Indian.

Many questions plagued me. I couldn't figure out why Alana hadn't returned to the ranch house. I wondered if she stayed away because she had felt unwanted, or if she was simply busy, or if she was deliberately trying to arouse my curiosity. The latter seemed closer to the truth, since she hadn't seemed to care when she imposed herself on me to gain a ride to the ranch. Why the mystery? For what purpose?

As I sat quietly contemplating the meaning of her invisibility, a wave of excited energy seemed to creep into the room and I began to feel that at any moment I would hear a rap at the door, or that she would appear as suddenly as she had disappeared. I recorded these impressions in my diary as possible psychic intrusions, reminding myself to "Be careful!", unsure if the woman's intention was to gain control of my land. Yet, as suspicious as I was, I also felt exhilarated by her invisible presence, and a part of me felt uplifted by the knowledge that she was on the property. Whenever I went for long walks across the land, I always expected to see her. A breeze rustling a bush would cause me to hesitate and look in that direction. I sometimes felt I heard her calling to the horses, or heard the sound of a horse's hoofs clapping against the ground, and I would become absolutely still to listen, but never did I see signs of her having been there.

CHAPTER TWO

THE CRACK IN
THE MOUNTAIN

I made a cup of tea, lit a fire in the fireplace, and then sat down at my desk to work. The early morning sun shone in through the window and warmed me, illuminating the screen on my portable computer. I began writing, noting sensations of lightness as I sat engrossed in the intricate weave of what I hoped would be the beginning of my new novel. Gradually, I became aware of the single beat of a drum. I paused to listen.

"Boom Boom Boom Boom Boom Boom Boom Boom" – and then it stopped. After a moment, it started again. I counted, eight drum beats in all, and then silence for a moment before it sounded again. Curious, I rose to my feet, went to the door, opened it, and looked out. At first I saw nothing but, as I was closing the door, the drum sounded again. I stepped outside onto the porch to listen, looking in all directions, at the hills and at the valley. It occurred to me that the sound may have been a boulder falling from the mountain, and I started to re-enter the house when I saw Alana coming toward me from the field. My heart raced. She was dressed in faded blue coveralls and red shirt, and she swayed as she walked. She carried a drum in one hand, and the other hung free at her side. As she approached, I could see she was smiling.

"Well, aren't you going to say hello to me?" she called from a short distance away.

"Hello Alana," I called back, aware of the morning chill on my arms. Something about her seemed different. She seemed younger somehow, and prettier, and there was a lightness about her that was both friendly and inviting.

She stood below the porch, grinning up at me. "Mind if I come up?"

"No, I don't mind," I said quickly.

Alana followed me inside, looked about the room, and then turned to me. I hesitated, relaxing as our eyes met.

"How have you been?" she asked, smiling at me.

"Just fine," I answered, still gazing into her eyes. I was very glad to see her.

She smiled, motioning to the well-lived-in room. "Looks cozy in here," she said. "Your uncle would've been happy to see you enjoying the place this way."

"Thanks," I said and smiled, a sudden surge of joy filling me. I wondered why.

"Got an extra cup of tea?" Alana asked, pointing to the cup on my desk.

"Sure," I said. "Sit down, I'll get you one."

She went to the couch to sit down and I went into the kitchen for the tea. I brought some cookies with me and put the cup and dish down on the burlwood table in front of the couch.

"Tell me what you think about the place," Alana said, sucking in the air with her tea to cool it as she sipped.

"It's beautiful," I answered.

"You've been all over the land, I suppose."

"Over much of it," I answered.

"Did you see the lake?"

"Yes."

"How about the river?"

"Yes, but not up close."

"Why not?"

"There hasn't been time," I answered, studying her interesting appearance. She seemed to be constantly changing, unlike anyone I had ever known.

"Have you found the hollow yet?" she asked, sipping her tea again and looking over the rim of her cup.

I shook my head. "Is it near the river?" I asked.

"Nope." She put her teacup on the table and lifted her drum onto her lap. It was a dug out section of tree with an animal skin stretched over the top. "You seen the horses?" she asked.

I hesitated, uneasy.

"What's the matter?" she asked.

"I thought I heard them a few times," I answered.

"You probably did."

"I could never be sure."

"They live near the hollow," Alana said. She looked directly at me and I felt a sudden warmth coming into me from her. "You're pretty," she said kindly.

I smiled, filled with the warmth of her presence. "Thanks," I answered.

She looked away, placing the drum on the table, then she leaned forward, the palms of her hands turned east and west on her knees. "Well, let's get down to business," she said matter-of-factly.

Her straightforwardness amused me and I waited for her to go on.

"First of all, do you want to be friends with me or not?" she asked, looking directly at me.

I shouldn't have been surprised but I was. "Yes, of course I do," I answered and I laughed.

"Good," she said, and paused, sticking out her lower lip as if considering what to say. She touched the drum with the fingers of her left hand and began to tap it. "I want to show you something," she said. "Put the palm of your hand on the drum, like mine."

I placed my hand on the opposite side of the drum from hers and watched as she raised her fingers and lightly thumped the surface. The vibration pulsed through my fingers. She stopped and looked at me.

"Did you feel it?" Alana asked.

"The vibration?"

"The energy," she answered. "I communicate through energy." She looked away and put the drum on the table, smoothing the top of it with her hand before she looked up again. "I am called Spirit Changer."

As I sat gazing into her eyes, I was struck by what she had not said. I suddenly realized that in the week I had not seen her she had been communicating with me through vibrations, or energy, as she called it, and I understood why I had been unable to tune her out of my consciousness. As long as I thought of her, had my attention on her, it was as though my fingers were on the drum.

"Do you understand the nature of energy?" Alana asked.

"I think so, Alana," I answered, looking away and then back at her again. I seemed to sink into them — the deep blue pools of her eyes, and I found an image of myself in them that startled me, although I couldn't identify what it was.

"How did you get the name Spirit Changer?" I asked nervously.

"It's my identity," Alana said, "I earned it you might say."

"In what way would you change someone?" I continued to prod.

"I do nothing," Alana went on. "It's a chemistry, the blending of one spirit with another spirit that effects change, and so what happens is not for me to say. Whatever change there is comes from what is ready to become." She paused, studying me. "Spirit is the essence of a person, but not a person's Soul. Guess that means my name is 'essence changer'." She laughed and then became serious again.

"Who named you Alana?"

"Life."

I hesitated, uneasily.

"The Indian way," Alana explained. "The Indian way uses signs from a person's life to find a name. The signs point to a person's nature."

While I was fascinated by her, I was also cautious, uncertain of her power.

"Heather, I didn't say my name had anything to do with you," Alana said, responding as though she understood my feeling. "I was just telling you what my name meant."

I was embarrassed, and rose to my feet. There was a long, deep silence between us, during which I wanted her both to leave and to stay. Then she rose to her feet as well. "You want to see the horses?" she asked. Instead of waiting for me to respond, she lifted the drum from the table and walked toward the door. I hesitated, then grabbed my sweater off the back of my desk chair as I followed her outside.

It was still early. The sun flickered in and out of a mountain pass, kissing the wet earth, beginning the slow, all-morning process of drying the tall, wet grass. My jeans were instantly wet, and I shivered in the morning chill. I was grateful that Alana walked quickly, cutting across the field to a deer trail that led through a meadow to the base of the mountain south of the house. She moved so swiftly that I was amazed at her agility. As I followed her through the tall, wet, gold and blue flowers and green grasses, I imagined her to be about half her age.

It wasn't the first time I had hiked that trail. Because of its well-traveled appearance, I had taken it to the base of the mountain several times, but each time I reached a dead end. It was a mystery to me why deer would cross a meadow only to turn around and come back the same way. While it may be natural for people to cut a trail to a scenic spot, it is not natural for animals. I spoke about this to Alana as we walked.

When I had finished speaking, Alana paused to turn and look at me. "You were right," she said, "the deer aren't stupid. They come up here to go into the hollow. You'll see." She continued walking to the far end of the meadow. The base of the mountain was overgrown with thick scrub bushes. She hesitated a moment and then turned and grinned at me. "This is where you stopped, isn't it?" she asked.

"Yes," I said noting the thorny cats-claw growing up against the mountainside.

"You were close, but not looking so good," Alana said kindly. She pointed to an outcropping of rock on the mountain directly ahead of us. "You didn't see the signs."

I scanned the protrusion, noticing that, while at first glance it looked one-dimensional, its flat appearance was really an illusion. For some reason I saw what I hadn't noticed before: the trail continued on the other side of the rocks.

Alana waited until I had discovered the way, then waved for me to follow her. She walked to the left of the protrusion to a passage that was about ten feet wide. "This crack in the mountain was formed during an earthquake when I was a little girl," she said. "Ever since then, the animals have used it to get into the hollow."

I went behind her and slipped behind the rocks. The passage was short, and a few steps later we entered a green grass meadow that extended as far as the eye could see to the next mountain range. A doe and her fawn grazed nearby undisturbed by our presence.

"It seems as though they don't see us," Alana whispered, "but they do. They don't run away, because they sense we mean them no harm."

I drew in a slow, deep breath, enchanted by the quiet beauty of the surroundings and the idea that we had entered a hidden valley that was probably unknown except to a few. "Is this the hollow?" I asked in a soft voice.

"Yes," Alana answered. "This is the hollow." She paused. "It got its name from your uncle, who called it the 'hollow of the world.' Your uncle Farley believed that this was a magic place, a place that was removed from the rest of the world."

"It does indeed appear that way," I said, looking out across a valley of wild flowers enclosed by sheer, blue-grey cliffs. It was a magnificent terrain.

Alana gathered up her coveralls in one hand, put the drum on the ground, and sat down beside it. "Now I'll show you how to call the horses," she said, motioning me next to her.

I sat down and rubbed my back against the rock wall. "It's so beautiful here," I whispered.

"Shhh, you must listen," Alana said. The doe and her fawn

looked up as we spoke, then lowered their heads and continued to graze.

I leaned against the cliff wall and sat still, listening as Alana had instructed. At first I heard only the birds and a trickle of wind through the tall grass and flowers, but then I became aware of a faint drumming sound, and I tensed, straining to listen deeper. Alana quietly put the drum on the ground in front of her and tapped it with open hands — slow, rhythmical drum beats pulsed into the environment. The deer lifted their heads, listened for a moment, and then bounded out of sight.

Alana quickened the beat, and the sound was like raindrops touching an open fire, a fascinating sound of released percussion smoldering into the air. She stopped after a moment, and listened. "Do you hear that?" she asked.

I listened. The sound of her drum seemed to continue even though she had stopped playing it.

"It's the horses," she whispered, and began to beat the drum again.

I leaned forward, caught by her excitement. Her playing was like pebbles being tossed into a pool. The sound spiraled outward, paused, and came back again in faint echo. Alana kept beating the drum, hesitating at rhythmical intervals, until suddenly she stopped and rose to her feet, leaving the drum on the ground. I leapt to my feet as well, frightened by a giant beat from the drum, but it wasn't the drum. A herd of maybe fifty horses raced across the hollow toward us. Alana motioned me to stay against the wall, and then stepped forward. The big lead stallion, a grey horse with a massive neck arched into the wind, galloped ahead, the others directly behind, as though they had no intention of stopping. Alana raised her right hand and stepped in front of them. My breath caught as I watched the great grey horse approach Alana, rear up on his hind legs to tower over her and then land a few feet directly in front of her. His nostrils flared with an odd twittering sound as he settled before her. The other horses came to a halt a short distance behind and then, as if they were accustomed to such meetings, settled into grazing. Alana reached up and stroked the leader's neck. Then, with a swoop of her shoulders, she lowered her neck and imitating the stallion's graceful walk, brought him up to me. I did not move.

"This is Stony," Alana said, smiling at my awed expression. "He is king of these wild horses and a very smart and wise king indeed." She ran her hand down the length of his nose. "Do as I do," she said. "When a horse looks you straight on and you stroke his face, you and he are saying hello."

I slowly raised my hand and ran it down the length of the great grey stallion's face. His nostrils flared as my hand passed over them.

"He knows your scent now," Alana said. "He will remember you when you meet again." She paused, reaching to stroke and pat his neck. "We are already friends, as you can see," she said, "although I think he likes me more than I do him."

Her response, touched with arrogance, surprised me, and I smiled.

"The mustangs are safe as long as they live on the back side of this mountain," Alana said, turning to look at the grazing herd some fifty or sixty yards back. Among them was a foal suckling at its mother's teat. "They live off the land. Grass is plentiful here, so humans have no reason to feel they have to control the size of the herd except greed." Alana fell silent, gazing into the vast terrain.

"Their secret is safe with me," I said reassuringly.

Alana stroked Stony's neck again and then looked at me. "Sometimes we don't mean to give things away," she said, "and we do it anyway."

"I will be careful," I said.

"Horses are different from us," Alana said, changing the subject. "They see differently, for one thing. If you ever approach the horses on your own, remember that."

I was fascinated. "I will," I answered.

"Be careful not to make quick movements," Alana continued. "Quick motion makes a flash of light in front of horses' eyes, and they'll run." She paused, crisscrossed her palms in front of her, and quickly brushed one with the other. Suddenly the grey stallion backed up, turned, and ran to join the herd. Alana turned to me again. "Did you see what happened?" she asked.

I was amazed and unsure. "I think so," I answered. "When you quickly brushed the palms of your hands together, the movement signaled the mustang to run off."

"Not the movement," Alana said, "the flash of light made from the movement. All life has a light around it, an energy field. The horses see this energy field. When there is sudden movement, the energy field shimmers and darts like lightening before their eyes. To horses, the movement of light is a warning signal." She fell silent again and watched the horses. The grey stallion lifted his head to look at her. "It's time for us to go," Alana said distantly, as though deep in thought. "I have other things to do today."

I hesitated, looking at her, fascinated by her unusual knowledge, and not wanting the moment to end. The concept of auras and psychic energy was not new to me, but I hadn't thought about it in relation to horses, nor did I have a clear working knowledge about how such energy manifested. I wished to know more, but before I could gather my thoughts to question her, Alana turned and started through the passageway. When she had led me to the other side, she paused and turned to face me. "We'll talk again soon," she said, as though she understood my curiosity, "but not today. I have things on the mountain I must do."

I started to ask what, but an inner nudge cautioned me not to prod. My experience had taught me to allow others to choose their time for telling about themselves. Instead I thanked her for the unusual demonstration with the horses and for showing me the hollow, and then I started down the hill. Halfway down, I turned and looked up to the base of the mountain again, but she had gone. As I gazed up at the place where I had last seen her, I suddenly felt the excitement of adventure, and young, and alive. I turned around and started for the house again, only now I skipped down the hill like a child.

When I reached the house, I burst through the doorway and went to my desk to sit down. There I spent the remainder of the day and the evening, drinking in memories of the Indian woman and of the experience in the hollow with the mustangs. I was fascinated by Alana's ability to communicate with them and in awe of her simple but powerful demeanor. In her presence I had felt her personal strength and vitality and, reflecting back, I again felt her magnetism, and was drawn to her, touched by ecstasy. I recalled how light and carefree I had felt after being with her.

I sat for hours updating my notes on Alana, and in them I recognized her as a new and powerful force in my life. However, because I didn't know what effect her chemistry would have on mine, I was also concerned that, if I was not careful, she might be able to project her ideas on to me. In some ways I already felt myself in her possession: because I was drawn by her unusual ability of communicating through energy, I had allowed her to think of my property as hers. I had accepted orders from her on my own land, in letting her dismiss me outside the hollow. I wanted to trust her because she was my uncle's friend. I also agreed with her that energy, as the producer of vibration, linked all life, and that fully realized it could revolutionize an individual's life or, as with the horses, an individual within the group and even the consciousness of the group as a whole.

These ideas shed new light on the book I was there to write. "Enter the Silence" or world without mind chatter, was beginning to reshape itself. I considered the title Alana had given me, "Between the Wind," certain that she would define the "wind" as energy. The title then would translate "between the energy." As I sat at my desk deep in thought, I knew she was thinking of me; that her energy was focused on me.

Later that night I awoke suddenly from a troubled sleep. It was shortly after midnight and, in the darkness, I sensed an electrical impulse, a wave of energy sweep over me. It was as though a presence had entered my bedroom and hovered over me. I pulled the sheets up over my head, but the intense feeling threatened to consume me. I thought of Alana and, in thought, accused her of trying to take possession of me.

I pushed the covers down and sat straight up in bed, then I turned on the light suddenly dispersing the darkness. As an experiment, I concentrated on pushing thoughts of Alana from me, but the more I pushed the stronger her image became. I cautioned myself to relax and to accept her being there, telling myself not to care if she was present, until I finally calmed myself by shifting my attention, observing her energy encompassing me, as meteorologists monitor a storm from the eye of the hurricane. For a time, I also imaged a protective white light surrounding me, but the feeling did not go away. As I lay in the darkness, a mentholated sensation settled in around my heart. Deep within I was convinced that Alana had somehow entered the deepest part of me. After some restlessness, I drifted into a troubled sleep.

The next morning shortly past dawn, there was a light rap at my door. I arose from my bed to answer it, knowing that it was Alana.

"Good morning," she said sweetly when I opened the door. "How was your night last night."

I hesitated as we looked into each other's eyes, and I thought of lying awake in the darkness. Now, as then, a mentholated feeling had settled in and around my heart. "Alana, I barely slept last night," I said finally.

She showed no change in expression.

"It was you who kept me awake," I offered boldly.

"How is that?" she asked.

"I don't know Alana, but I could feel your presence in my room. It awakened me," I said.

"What did you feel?" she asked curiously.

As I told her about the sensation around my heart, and the feeling that she was possessing me, I suddenly felt stupid.

"I am only being myself," she said. "I don't do anything. I just am, I BE. It is you who keep yourself awake."

I was annoyed, although most of my annoyance was directed at myself for not being more clever in my speech. "But your being intrudes," I retorted angrily. "I did not invite your feelings." I knew what I had said wasn't true, that I had projected both curiosity and skepticism toward her.

Alana hesitated, then sighed. "You tell me, Heather," she said, "what the rules of our friendship are. You set them and I will abide by them."

I stared at her, knowing that I had been both unkind and foolish. "Never mind," I said, apologetically shrugging my shoulders, "Let's drop it. There can be no rules to a friendship."

Alana nodded, then said that she was on her way to the mountain and would speak with me another time. As I shut the door behind her, butterflies seemed to settle in my solar plexus and creep upward toward my heart. The mentholated feeling stayed with me and I suddenly felt lonely.

I spent the rest of the day making notes about my experiences with Alana and, when I could think of nothing more to write, I went for a walk across the valley, trying not to think about her. A thin, high-pitched musical note occasionally sounded in my inner ear.

That night I was again awakened shortly after midnight, tormented by Alana's presence, and I felt resentful, and resistant to her.

The next morning shortly past dawn there was again a rap at the door. I rose and opened it abruptly.

"It's a beautiful morning," Alana said sweetly, "and on the way over here, I saw three deer standing beneath a rainbow."

I was caught off guard by the beautiful imagery of her words. "That must have been a wonderful sight," I answered.

"It was." She paused. "Did you sleep well?" she asked.

I stared at her. "Alana," I said feeling foolish, "I barely slept at all. I keep feeling your presence and it keeps me awake."

She made a "what do I do now" expression. "Do you feel all right?" she asked. "I mean, are you tired?"

I shook my head, suddenly aware that, while I hadn't slept more than two hours during the last couple of nights, I felt strong and energized. "I feel really good," I answered, chuckling to myself.

Alana smiled. "That is good," she said, then she excused herself, saying that she had to go and would talk to me later.

In the days that followed I read and reread my notes about Alana and the uncertainty she inspired. I was deeply concerned that she was practicing a form of black magic and was trying to take total possession of me but, at the same time, I argued that black magic would give me negative sensations rather than the ecstasy and super energy I felt. I decided that if I could discover the reason for her attention, her intent, then I could relax. I decided to avoid her until I could be sure.

One morning, before the time that I felt Alana would arrive, I drove into town. It was a light, airy morning, filled with the scent of pine and lavender, and I drove the Jeep as fast as I could and still keep the noise from the wind flaps under bearable control. Forty minutes later, I pulled up in front of the general store and stepped out of the Jeep. The proprietor was hurrying to finish sweeping the porch before opening, but he paused to greet me.

"Howdy," he said.

"Howdy."

"How's the Farley place?"

"Just beautiful!" I answered.

He nodded, eyeing me uncertainly, and then went inside, leaving the door open.

I walked over to the counter, paused and then began to look at everything, from soup to nuts, in its plainest form. There was very little commercially prepared food on the shelves. "I need some eggs," I said, "and some tea, chamomile, if you have it."

He gave me a peculiar look.

"Any herb tea will be fine," I said.

He reached up and retrieved the items from the shelf and placed them on the countertop, looking at me.

"I guess that's all," I said, "unless you have some oranges."

"How many ya want?" he asked, reaching for his half-spectacles from next to the cash register.

"About a dozen."

He put on his glasses, turned away, and disappeared into the back room momentarily; he returned with a sack of oranges. "That it?"

"Yes," I said.

"That'll be $7.28," he said.

I reached in my pocket, drew out a ten-dollar bill, and handed it to him. He rang up the sale and handed me the change. "Is Alana out there with you?" he asked.

I looked at him as I took the money. "She's not with me," I said, "but I see her on occasion."

"That so," he said.

"That's so," I repeated.

"She always lived with old man Farley," the proprietor said, trying to be nonchalant.

"That so," I said, mimicking him.

"I guess you're too busy writin' to have someone around full time," he said. "I never read your books but I heerd some things about them."

"Yes, I am busy," I said, taking up my bag of groceries. I smiled again and left the store.

On the way back to the ranch I thought about my visit to the grocery store and the proprietor's reference to Alana, wondering if she had mentioned me to him or if he had been merely fishing for my reaction to her. What interested me most of all was my own obsessive interest in her. I felt sure that she was projecting images of herself to me; that she was using me to some end or setting me up to use me. I thought about her constantly.

When I drove up in front of the house, Alana was sitting on the steps, waiting. She waved. A sharp edge of uneasiness suddenly pushed into my heart as I drew the Jeep to a halt and got out with the bag of groceries.

"Today's a special day in the hollow," Alana said, rising.

"It is?" I asked, jolted by surprise.

She nodded.

"I had an important dream last night," Alana said.

Believing that her dream might shed some light on why she haunted me, I looked at her curiously. "What was it?" I asked.

"Heather," she said, "I was driving a car, my car." She hesitated, allowing the silence to confirm my belief that she did not have a car and had never driven one. "All of a sudden, I looked up at the sky and saw clouds collecting over my head. I started to drive faster but some great force picked up my car and tipped it over on its side. I turned and looked out the window and I caught a glimpse of what it was that had struck me." She hesitated, looking distantly into space.

"What was it?" I prodded, momentarily forgetting my uneasiness.

"Lightening! A bolt of lightening had come down from the highest place in the heavens and struck my vehicle," Alana said.

"Your vehicle," I repeated, mulling her story over in my mind. "It sounds as if the lightening was a message from the inner worlds."

We stared at each other for a long moment until she began nodding her head. "Yes," she said, "I know that is true, Heather."

I looked away, aware of a deep feeling passing from her to me and returning again. There was no way I could deny to myself that I was drawn to her; that I was in some unexplainable way becoming more and more attached to her. To my surprise, the feeling humbled me.

"Do you want to go with me to the hollow?" she asked.

"I do Alana, but I have so much work to do," I answered, feeling that I should detach myself from her, but wanting to go.

She hesitated, then nodded and turned away, starting toward the mountain. As I watched her leave, I was overcome by the desire to go with her. I knew that if I stayed home to work I would accomplish little.

"Alana, wait!" I called.

Alana stopped and turned around.

"I want to go with you," I said. "Let me put the groceries in the house and I will be right out."

"The illusion has been made
to look like the real
Just as the real is made
to look as if it did not exist.

The Sea is covered,
but the Foam is shown;
The Wind is concealed from sight,
yet the Dust is manifest."

RUMI

CHAPTER THREE

THE NATURE OF INDIVIDUAL REALITIES

As I followed Alana up the hillside, I wondered if I *really* wanted to be there with her or if her influence over me was so strong that she had *made* me want to be there. I argued the point within myself, feeling silly for having thought it, yet reminding myself that I had driven into town to miss her daily morning visit only to find her waiting for me when I returned. Did I really want to see her after all? I knew that my curiosity had been aroused, and I also knew that curiosity could be a powerful trigger into the unknown.

Alana turned, looked at me, and grinned as if she knew what I had been thinking; then she continued on up the hill again.

I thought about her smile. I believed it reflected a knowingness about me, as if she was letting me know that she was gradually consuming me and could see directly into me. Butterflies stirred in my solar plexus, a sign that, according to occultists, meant the intrusion of another person's emotional energy. Why was I allowing it?

Alana paused before the outcropping of rocks by the passage and turned to face me. "This time, you go first," she said kindly. There was a light in her eyes that seemed to reach out and touch me around my heart. I went ahead of her.

An ethereal mist hung over the hollow, adding a mystical beauty to the grandeur. I didn't see any wildlife, not deer, nor horses, nor anything else. Then, off to the north, I noticed a circular opening in the mist. I gave Alana a questioning glance. She nodded that I should go on. I started across the grassy meadow toward the hole in the mist. Alana stayed close behind me. Suddenly I stopped, fascinated, watching as the mist rolled back and a doorway formed in it. Unsure, I turned again to face Alana. She motioned that I should go ahead. Cautiously, I stepped through the doorway to the other side.

Just ahead the sun was shining on a group of people seated around an enormous crystal: it must have been three feet high and at least a foot in diameter.

Alana came alongside me and motioned me forward. As I stepped closer I heard a thin, high-pitched sound, like a single note of a flute, only I saw no instruments being played. I remained still, listening, taken by the dramatic pitch of one long note followed by another, thinking at first that the musical sound came from the crystal, or that the crystal was a conductor or amplifier for it. I turned to Alana for an explanation.

"Be sure of what you see, Heather," she whispered.

I turned again to gaze at the crystal and those gathered about it. The thin, high-pitched flute sound was so intense that it touched me deeply. There was an intense lightness around my heart and I remembered that thinking about Alana had caused that same reaction over the last few days. It occurred to me that the feeling indicated that my heart center was open. In a moment of giddy ecstasy, I turned to her and smiled.

My heart leapt as her eyes met mine. Somewhere inside I heard myself tell her that I accepted her; that I knew she was a spiritual teacher.

"Take note of what you see here," Alana reminded me softly.

I turned to the gathering again, noting that the people were young and old, men and women and children. They appeared to be totally involved and did not notice Alana or me.

"Be sure!" Alana prodded softly.

The scene began to fade. Gradually, the mist crept into the circle obscuring the people and making the crystal imperceptible.

"What happened?" I asked, staring into the mist.

"Tell me what you saw," Alana urged.

I was unsure, and slow to speak, and then I told her what I had seen.

"Really?" she asked.

"Yes, really," I answered, turning to look at her. The question in her voice took me by surprise.

"That is not what I saw at all," she said in a quiet voice.

"What do you mean?"

"I mean we did not see the same thing."

I didn't know what to say and stood motionless, studying her, waiting for her to go on.

"Heather, you seem to think that we all see the same things in life," Alana said.

"To a point," I answered. "There is a certain reality that we all tend to see."

Alana drew in a deep breath and turned away, as if to consider what she wished to tell me, then she looked at me again. "People's realities are quite different from each other, much more so than you realize."

While I was sure that was true, I didn't understand how it related to what we were discussing.

"Even though we were looking in the same direction," Alana said, "we did not see the same thing."

"I don't understand what you mean," I said impatiently, believing that I had observed something she had missed. "Of course, our individuality made us see differently."

"And there you have it," Alana said, pausing to look deeply at me. "I did not see people gathered about a crystal. I saw two circles of stones, one circle within another circle. There was no mist."

I was too astounded to speak.

"It is true," she said, watching me.

"But there were people — men, women and children," I said.

"Only in your eyes," Alana said, "not mine."

I was dumbfounded as I looked across the distant, misty terrain. For an instant I thought I saw the movement of something invisible through it. I wondered if Alana was trying to trick me, and why.

"Don't try to confuse me with your scenario," Alana said harshly, watching me scan the terrain.

I turned to face her. Her deep-set, dark blue eyes first glared at me threateningly, and then softened. I wondered if she knew what I had been thinking.

"Heather," she said, speaking my name in a gentle voice.

"Yes."

"You do understand the nature of illusion," she said

questioningly.

"Yes," I said, nodding." All individuals live according to their state of consciousness."

"Exactly," Alana said.

"But there is also a general reality to life," I added.

"Only by agreement," Alana said.

There was a long moment in which neither of us spoke.

"When I told you it was a special day in the hollow and invited you to join me here, the agreement between us to see and experience the same thing was broken. You believed there would be something special, out of the ordinary, and since I gave you no indication of what the specialness would be, your consciousness decided what it was. You have a very vivid imagination." Alana grinned at me.

Although still unable to concede the point, I was embarrassed by the idea that my imagination could have run away with me.

"It's what makes you a creative writer," Alana said, as if aware of my embarrassment. "You made a strange and unusual story from your imagination. If you sold real estate instead, your imagination would have been parceling the hollow into little sections to sell for profit."

Her analogy made sense to me. "But what about the common reality among people," I said thoughtfully.

"The only common reality that exists is the place," Alana explained. "The nature of the place and what it looks like varies from person to person, except those parts about which a common agreement has been made."

I started to argue but she hushed me.

"When you speak of understanding individual realities," Alana went on, "your mind is not following. If it were, you would have no questions about what I have said."

I was flabbergasted by the certainty with which she spoke. Her statements were true, of course, and that made me feel not only threatened but also angry.

"You believe yourself to be a very flexible person," Alana went on, "while in reality you are one of the most inflexible people I have ever met."

"That's not true!" I argued.

Alana stood motionless, studying me. "Heather, when you don't like something, you move things around to find another way of dealing with it."

"Right," I said proudly.

"That's what I mean."

"What do you mean?" I asked.

"Flexibility is when everything is okay as it is," Alana said. "When you accept change, you are being flexible. Trying to change everything around to have it the way you want it is being inflexible.

"Another thing that I instinctively know about you," Alana continued, "is that you use kindness to another person to effect change."

"I suppose I do," I answered confidently, pleased that she could find something about me to praise.

"Pushing a kindness button does not make one flexible," Alana said, drawing in a deep breath. "All it does is make you a manipulator. You manipulate people to suit yourself."

"I do not!"

"When you found that I was going to the ranch, whether you wanted me there or not," she said, "you pushed the button of kindness toward me, thinking you would have to try that way of handling me."

I looked away uneasily.

"When I left you at the ranch house you became suspicious that I was plotting against you."

"That's not true!" I asserted again, ashamed that she knew what I had been feeling about her.

She stared at me, nodding her head up and down as if thinking over what she would say next. "You believe that I have been trying to manipulate you, to control you through psychic energy, when in truth it is you who have been trying to control me."

I wanted to run away but held my ground. "I can feel you coming psychically in on me, even in the middle of the night; you wake me up," I said.

"You do it all to yourself," she said calmly, studying me as if I were some sort of peculiar specimen.

"What about the pain in my solar plexus, and the mentholated sensation around my heart?" I asked.

"What about it?"

"I didn't do that to myself," I proclaimed.

"You didn't?"

"No."

She eyed me from the bottom of my toes to the top of my head. "Another thing," she said. "You're a proclaimer, Heather. You are always proclaiming this and that. In other words, Heather, you are a grandstander, and your manner of doing it proves my point. Your grandstanding behavior is merely another display of your inflexibility."

I was dumbfounded and hurt. I certainly did want to argue with her. It was obvious that I was at a terrible disadvantage; she was not going to leave my property and she knew it better than I did. I simply had to see it though until I could learn the land from her. She was not going to show her hand until she was ready. I had to put up with her.

She made a strange and sudden movement: she sort of sniffed the air around her, and her head shook slightly and rhythmically. She seemed to be in a state of unusual alertness. She spun around and then stared at me with a look of bewilderment and curiosity. Her eyes swept up and down my body as if she were looking for something specific; then she abruptly began to walk fast. She was almost running. I followed her as she started through the passageway, but she stopped abruptly as if she had seen something terrible blocking our path, and turned onto a path between two rock walls that I had not noticed before. I hurried after her. She kept up a very fast pace for nearly half an hour.

Finally we reached the river and she stopped. We sat in the shade of a pine tree. The trotting had exhausted me completely, although my mood was better. The change in the way I felt was strange. I was almost elated, but when we started to hurry, after our argument, I was furious with her.

"I can't believe it," I said, "but I really feel good."

A pine cone fell from the branch just above us and landed in front of me. She turned and smiled to me.

"That was an omen," she said.

I heard a hawk screech in the distance.

She laughed out loud and pointed in the direction of the sound. "And that was an agreement," she said.

She then asked me if I was ready to talk about my inflexibility. I laughed. My anger seemed so far away that I could not imagine how I had become so furious with her.

"I don't know what's happening to me," I said. "I was angry and I don't know why I'm not any more."

"Life is very mysterious," she said. "It doesn't reveal its secrets easily."

I liked her enigmatic statement. It was challenging and

mysterious. I couldn't be sure if it was filled with hidden meaning or not.

"If you ever come this way by yourself," Alana said, "stay away from this tree where we rested today. Avoid it like a disease."

"Why? What's the matter?"

"This is not the time to talk about it," she said. "Now we are concerned with being flexible. As long as you feel that you must change things to suit yourself you cannot enter between the wind. You are like the victim of a crime, or of social prejudice, or even the weather. There is no freedom in inflexibility."

She examined me a moment.

"I am going to visit with my little friend here," she said, pointing to a scorpion on a small rock near her foot.

She kneeled in front of it, bent down, and began to talk to it. I could not make out what she was saying, and she started to laugh. Then she stood up.

"The scorpion just told me a story," she said. "It isn't the words that count in the telling of a story, but the energy behind it."

She told me that the scorpion told her that it had asked a frog to carry it on its back across the river. The frog was afraid that the scorpion would sting it, but the scorpion assured the frog that kindness would be repaid with friendship. Alana hesitated before finishing the story, looking at me in a most compassionate way.

I felt uneasy but kept quiet, waiting for her to go on.

"When the frog had delivered the scorpion to this side of the river," Alana said, "the scorpion stung it."

"Why? What for?"

Alana gestured with her hands raised open in front of her. "The scorpion had no choice."

"Why?" I asked again.

"Its nature is to sting," Alana said apologetically.

"But it promised the frog," I said, full of emotion.

"It promised the frog," she said, "but the promise was inflexible, against its nature. The scorpion pushed a kindness button in frog to get to the other side."

"But why should frog have been the victim?" I asked. "He pushed a kindness button in taking scorpion across the river."

"True," she said, "but pushing someone's kindness buttons is the inflexible way. Frog was not being true to himself in taking scorpion across the river."

"What do you mean?

"Frog knew of the dangers."

I was upset and shifted uneasily from foot to foot in an effort not to voice what I was feeling about the story. It seemed to me that frog had been done an injustice.

"Each of us can only be what we are," Alana said. "When we are anything else, we become inflexible."

Alana patted me on the back and said that it was all right, that at least I would begin to realize my own inflexibility and to correct it.

"From now on, be aware of the nature of other forms of life," she said, "including other human beings and don't expect them to be anything other than themselves. Remember the flexible way is when everything is okay, when you can accept what is or what isn't."

She went on to tell me that she could look at a situation or a person and immediately see whether it or the individual was flexible or not. Inflexible people were usually argumentive and willful.

I interrupted that I believed that willful people were those who directed their own lives rather than have someone else direct their lives for them.

"That is both true and untrue," Alana said, watching me. "You are very willful, but your willfulness is lived in a very inflexible way. When you can be willful and content at the same time, then your willfulness will work for you instead of against you. Another thing," she said, pausing as if to make sure I was listening, "you have a way of flip-flopping back and forth in your emotions."

I felt a bit defensive and asked her to explain herself.

"Another time," she said curtly, "I cannot educate you all in one day."

That statement sunk me into the depths of embarrassment. How could it be possible for such an uneducated woman, a person who had lived so out of sorts with the world, to teach me the values of life and how to change the shortcomings in myself? I thought I was educated and aware and yet she obviously knew more than I did.

She began to walk downriver. I followed her.

I felt elated. I was very happy walking inanely after the strange Indian woman. She paused and looked at me but did not say a word.

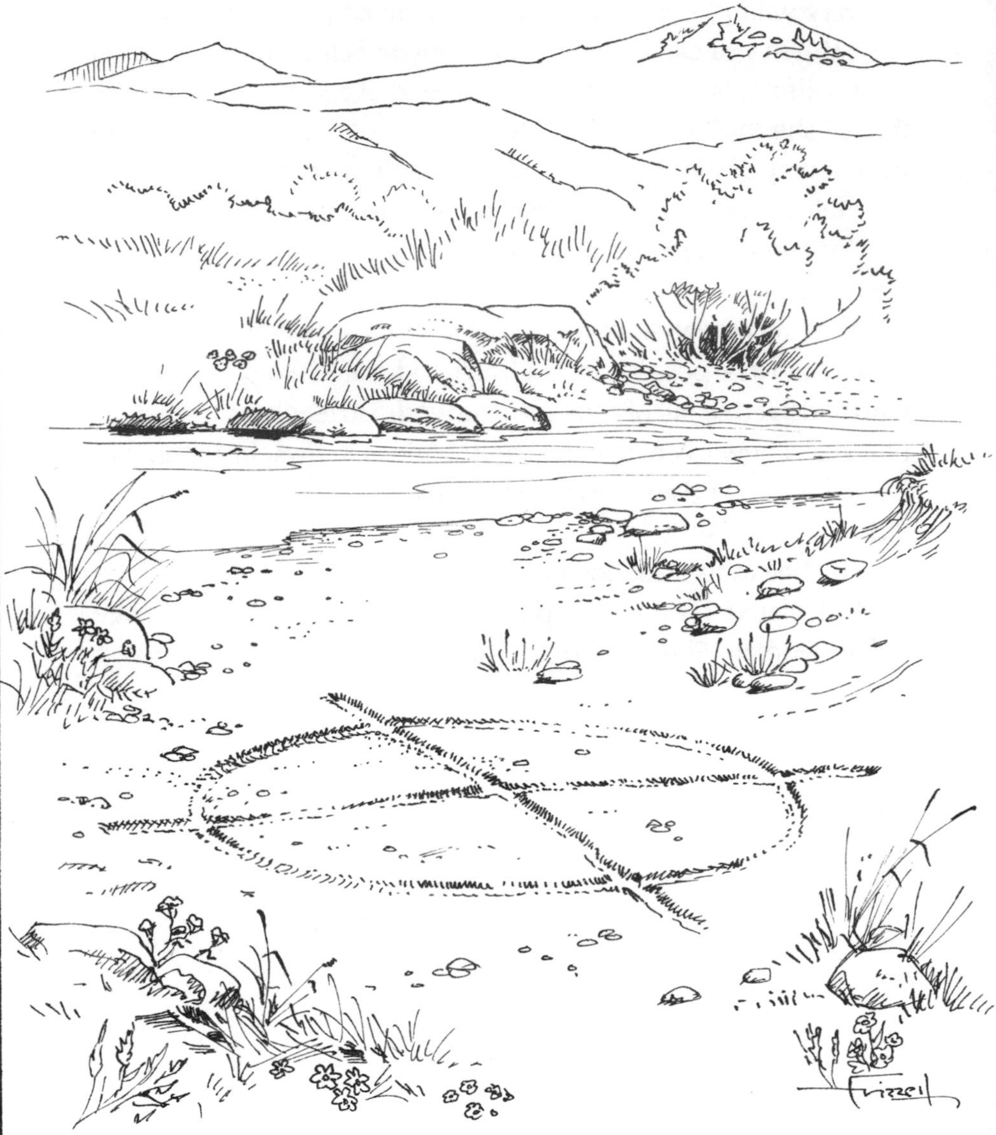
Frizzell

CHAPTER FOUR
THE ILLUSION OF WILLFULNESS

"**W**ould you teach me someday about the mentholated heart?" I asked.

She did not answer and, as she had done before, looked at me as if I were crazy.

When I had mentioned the sensation to her, during our discussion on inflexibility, she smiled and shook her head. The gesture was not affirmative or negative; it was rather a gesture of amusement and disbelief.

She stood up abruptly. We had been sitting on the porch steps in front of the house. A subtle movement of her head invited me to follow her.

We went west into the meadow. She repeated as we walked that I had to be aware of my resistance to flexibility, that I was constantly wanting to control the direction we were going.

I knew better than to argue with her. It was true that I believed that she was leading me to the river and that I kept trying to go the way I had gone to it before. Each time we started toward the river, she changed to a parallel direction and I would catch myself stumbling in an uncoordinated effort to stay with her.

"Your friends," she said, turning to me abruptly. "Those who have known you for a long time, you must leave them quickly."

I thought she was crazy and her insistence was idiotic, but I did not say anything. She peered at me and began to laugh.

"I did not mean people friends," Alana explained, "I meant those negative attitudes and addictions, habits, that you have been carrying with you a long time. You are so accustomed to them that you treat them like friends. You must leave them quickly."

I suddenly felt like I was walking alongside of her with no clothes on and no way to hide myself. I said nothing.

After a rather long distance we stopped on a hill just above the river. I was about to sit down to rest but she told me to wait. She walked a few paces away and drew a large circle on the ground just below where I was standing, then she called up to me. "Can you see it?"

"The circle, yes," I called back.

"Sit down and see if you can still see it," she instructed.

I sat and gazed down at the circle. By now she was deepening it with a stick, gouging the lines to make the circle stand out stronger, then she drew another line through it from north to south and another from east to west. The river ran some twenty paces behind it, and an occasional piece of wood or branch of leaves floating past gave a feeling of motion to the circle. I thought of the other afternoon in the hollow and the illusions that I had confronted, and I wondered if I was about to have a similar experience.

"You wanted to learn about your willfulness and the illusion it produces," Alana said, moving midway up the hill between where I sat and the circle.

I wondered if she actually knew what I was thinking most of the time or if I was tuned in on *her* mental process, but I kept quiet.

"The circle I have drawn is the medicine wheel," she said, pointing with her stick downhill at the circle she had drawn. "The two lines drawn through it break the circle into the four directions."

She glared at me in a way that demanded my attention. I didn't like feeling subordinate to her. She had such a strong overbearing manner about her, and I knew that one of us would have to yield. I also knew it would be me.

"The four directions are the east, west, north and south," Alana said looking at me. "The east is the direction of spiritual energies; the west stands for introspection. If you want to mull something over, the west is the direction for your attention. South is for happy thoughts and activities, adventure. North is for wisdom. Do you follow me?" she asked.

I started to question her but decided against it. "Yes," I answered, "I have seen the medicine wheel drawn in books about Shamanism."

She glared at me again, and I suddenly wished that I had kept my mouth shut. Why did I feel it necessary to make her think that I knew something, when what I knew about the medicine wheel was very little, book knowledge that had little strength next to the practical knowledge she was about to offer me.

"I want you to choose a direction," she said. "When you've chosen a direction, take a deep breath and *relax*. Face straight ahead. Let your vision be diffused, don't really look at anything. This is what is called soft eye, or soft vision. Note that when you are using soft eyes, you are not looking hard at any one thing, but see the environment as a whole. In this way the mind will become quiet and you will find yourself listening, inwardly listening. After a moment or two, turn your head to the east." She paused, using the stick in her left hand to point to the east on the medicine wheel. "Note your impressions from that soft eye flow. See where the experience leads you."

I wished that I had a notebook with me and said so.

"You don't need to write anything down," she said. "The impressions you receive will be recorded deeply within you, within the moment of their conception. To recall them at any time in the future, you will need only to recall the moment, the feeling of the moment in which they occurred. Do you understand me?"

I was astounded and pleased. I had always felt that anything once received by the senses was indelible, like an invisible ink that becomes visible when held up to the light. "I understand," I answered.

"Then begin," she instructed.

I took a deep breath and tried to relax as she instructed. My vision diffused while I looked east, and I experienced what she called "soft eyes," and saw the environment as a whole. The river flowed not behind the circle as before but became a part of the medicine circle, blending the brown from the water to the brown of the earth, the green of the foliage on the river bank with the green branches overhanging the circle, while the movement of the water seemed to animate the earth and the earth seemed to slow the movement of the water.

After a moment, Alana asked me what direction I had chosen for my soft eyes and what I had seen, and I told her. She didn't speak for what seemed a long time. "You have had an experience of energy blending," she said finally. "Do you know what that means?"

"No," I said, anxious to hear what she would say.

She shook her head. "I cannot tell you that now," she said. "It is not time."

"What do you mean?" I was disappointed.

"Just that," she said. "When it is time, we will talk about it."

"Alana," I said, upset and unable to control my sense of urgency. I felt that what she knew was important to the book I was writing. "I want to know now. It's important that I know now."

She shook her head and looked away, toward the river.

I became frustrated and angry. "Alana, you can't just show me something and then leave it hanging like that."

She slowly turned her head, glaring at me.

"I'll pay you!" I said emphatically. "This way we'll both feel better. I could then ask you anything I want to because you would be compensated for it. What do you say?"

She looked at me contemptuously and made an ugly sound with her mouth, pursing her mouth to vibrate and spit between her lips with force.

"I am not for sale," she said, and laughed uproariously at the total surprise that must have shown on my face.

It was obvious to me that she was not someone I could easily persuade. Her demeanor went from simplicity to a great power that constantly surprised me. I decided to appeal for help to the gentler side of her nature.

"It would help me to learn about energy blending now," I said pleadingly. "Not that I really believe that it is anything that I don't already know, but the Indian perspective of it is unknown to me and I would really appreciate it if you would share a bit of your wisdom with me."

She let out a howl and sat on the ground burying her face in her hands. For a moment I didn't know whether she was crying or laughing, but then I realized that she was doubled up in laughter.

I felt offended and insulted after the plea for help I had made to her. "Why are you laughing at me?" I asked.

She sat up straight and looked at me. "Heather, you think you can flatter me into working for you. I told you in the very beginning that I would work *with* you; that I wanted no payment in return."

"Then help me understand what it is about energy blending that I need to know," I said.

"You really don't know what you're saying, do you?" she asked.

I didn't answer. I sensed she was laying a trap for me and I was already too vulnerable.

"You are very strong, Heather," she said without expression.

I took her statement as a compliment and relaxed a bit, waiting for her to continue.

She studied me in silence, a peculiar smile upturning her lips.

"I don't know how to tell you," Alana said hesitantly.

"Just say it," I prodded. I felt empowered by her description of me as strong.

She rose, turned, and looked as far back over her shoulder as she could, but instead of looking straight back into the distance, she was looking down at her rump. "Can you tell what I am looking at?" she asked.

"I think so," I answered, leaning forward and to the side.

"You try it," she said, turning back to me.

I rose to my feet, turned as she had done and looked back over my shoulder and down toward my rump. "Do you mean the buttocks?" I asked uneasily.

She let out a yell and doubled over as though she was in pain.

I was frightened and believed that something might be wrong with her, and then I realized that she was laughing at me.

"You still don't get it, do you?" she asked with some difficulty through her laughter.

"Get what?" I asked, annoyed.

She turned back and stared at her buttocks again. She patted them with her hand and then pointed to me. It occurred to me suddenly that she was calling me an ass and I straightened, indignant at the idea.

"All right," she said apologetically, "I will help you. But you must pay strict attention to what I am about to say."

"I will."

"Good, then we will begin," she said. "Your first lesson in energy blending is to learn the art of flexibility."

Since we had already discussed that subject at greater length than I had liked, I didn't ask what she meant.

"One cannot blend energies with anyone or anything when they are inflexible," she went on. "Don't you see, Heather, when you try to convince me that I should tell you something that I have already said would have to wait, you are displaying willfulness, and such willfulness is inflexibility."

I realized why she had been laughing at me; that she hadn't intended to compliment my personal strength by calling me strong. "But how else will I learn what I want to know if I don't ask you to tell me?" I prodded.

"Life cheats no one," Alana said. "If we believe ourselves cheated, it is because of our inattention."

"What do you mean?" I asked. I felt I was paying strict attention to every detail of the time we spent together.

"Your medicine wheel vision merely opens the door to a life experience," she said. "It is the life experience that follows that is the true explainer. I can only offer you images and direction, but life will teach you in a way you will never forget."

I was humbled by her explanation, but still impatient to gather the knowledge I wanted.

"Do you recall how your energy blending vision came to you?" Alana asked.

"You said soft vision," I answered.

She nodded slowly and repeatedly. "Yes, yes, soft vision," she said. "And it comes as a result of relaxation, of allowing the vision to diffuse. You must begin to view life more and more in this manner until gradually you witness the blending of all energies."

"...when you try to convince me
that I should tell you something that
I have already said will have to wait,
you are displaying willfulness, and
such willfulness is inflexibility."

CHAPTER FIVE

BLENDING OF THE ENERGIES

The next morning I awoke at dawn and hurriedly dressed myself. Since I expected Alana to arrive at any moment, I went out onto the front porch and waited for her, gazing at the base of the thick range of mountains and wondering where she was. I had grown accustomed to her early morning visits and I planned my days around them. Her presence in my life had changed the direction of the book I was writing; her breath was the essence of it.

After a time I grew impatient, and thought that there had to have been some reason why she had not come. I considered that something might be wrong and decided to set out to look for her.

I packed a few pieces of fruit in a day pack, which I tied around my waist, and then set out for the river. It seemed the logical place to find her because it was where we had last met.

I took the shortcut she had shown me and cut quickly through the west meadow. It wasn't long before I stood on the hill above the river, looking down on the spot where Alana had drawn the medicine wheel on the dirt bank. Not seeing her, I started to turn away, to look for her in another direction, when something shiny caught my attention. Close to the spot where she had drawn the medicine wheel was something that was mysteriously bright.

I bent my knees and slid down the hill on my haunches, my feet twisting this way and that as though they were on skis. Just above the medicine wheel Alana had drawn I came to a stop and stood up. There in the center was a large white shiny stone. It looked like a polished moonstone. I immediately decided that Alana had placed it there as a sign or symbol for me. She must have known that I would look for her there.

Filled with a sense of mystery and adventure, I gazed at the stone and noticed that a circle had been drawn in the dirt around it. Extending from the circle was a line that pointed west. I turned and looked in that direction. Almost instantly a flash of bright light was mirrored on the side of the hill. It was in direct line, or so it seemed, with the moonstone on the ground in front of me. I headed in that direction.

When I arrived on the side of the hill, I found another moonstone. Again there was a circle drawn around it, and again there was a line pointing from the circle, but this one pointed north. I looked that way. Because of the direction of the sunlight I didn't see anything for a time, but then I noticed a bright spot of light farther up on a rock ledge. The ledge appeared rather steep, and I was unsure if I should try to check it out or not. I sat down and ate an apple as I thought about it. If Alana had placed the stone up there, I could surely climb up to the spot as well. I set out for the ledge.

I felt youthful and strong as I pulled myself up onto the rock ledge and found the third moonstone. Out of breath, I brushed the dirt from my jeans, looked out across the terrain, and then sat down, picking up the stone and turning it around in my hands. It appeared to be just an ordinary stone. The underside was caked with dirt while the top was smooth and shiny. Its coloring was different from the others and I couldn't be sure if it was a moonstone or not, but I assumed it was. I put it back where I had found it and noticed a line running from north to south. From this high point I could see the moonstone nearest the river and the one I had just left on the side of the hill, and I saw what appeared to be a fourth stone almost directly across from me. It seemed that Alana had placed a stone in the four directions of the medicine wheel, but to what purpose?

As I sat and looked from one direction to another, from stone to stone, I recalled Alana's earlier instruction to choose a "looking" direction and to gaze with relaxed vision into it. I thus became aware of the valley and mountains all around me, realizing that I could see almost the full 360 degrees. I perceived the mountainside behind me, in detail that wasn't possible while using my normal vision. Mostly I became aware of the slightest movement of things, the flutter of a bird or the slight bend of the tall grass in a gentle breeze and there seemed to be a halo around all life. I felt absolutely at peace, without a thought or opinion about what I was experiencing.

Later that morning I returned home to find Alana waiting for me on the porch.

"Good morning Alana," I said. "I am sure glad I found you!"

She softly laughed. Her eyes swept over me as though she were taking account of all the dirt I had accumulated on my clothes.

I sat down on the porch next to her. "That was sure some

demonstration you set up for me," I said, trying to contain my excitement.

"What demonstration?" She turned her head slightly and then her full body to see me better. "What are you talking about?"

"You know, the moonstones," I said assuredly.

"What moonstones?"

"The medicine circle you drew down by the river, the stone there and those you planted in all four directions from it," I said, anxious to tell her what I had learned.

"Heather, I don't know what you're talking about," she said. "I didn't place any stones anywhere."

She seemed so sincere I didn't know what to say next, and I remembered the singing crystal I had seen in the hollow that she said had not been there.

"You sure have a vivid imagination," she added, studying me.

I shook my head. "The stones were not my imagination," I said. I then explained how I had gone to each of the stones and had felt the blending of energies from the medicine wheel, had seen the blending of those energies with my soft vision and the soft halo of light that engulfed it all.

"Isn't that wonderful," Alana said after a time, and smiled at me.

"Yes, it was very wonderful," I said, relieved.

"But Heather, you must know I had nothing to do with any of it," she said. "What you experienced was of your own making. I did not set it up for you."

I believed she was trying to trick me and so I didn't say anything.

Alana rose to her feet, walked down the porch steps, and stopped a short distance away. She was looking at the ground. "Come here, Heather," she called, motioning me to her.

I went over and looked at the ground where she was looking. There was a stone and it appeared that there had been a circle drawn around it; then I saw that it was really a shadow. Coming out of the shadow was a straight line pointing east. I didn't know what to make of what I was seeing until I realized that the line pointing to the east had not been drawn there but was a natural line in the earth's surface. It could have just as easily been a straight line created by the shadow of a tree branch. I was embarrassed, and did not know what to say.

"You are an easy student," Alana said not unkindly, "because when I make a suggestion you teach yourself. And that is fine, except that you miss the point of what I am trying to teach you." She paused to study me, then added, "How is it that you are a writer and yet you express yourself in a very limited way to me?"

I looked at her uneasily, unsure whether she was taunting me or if what I had experienced was truly valid. Then I described to her how I often felt when she talked to me and how incongruous it was for me to be tongue-tied.

She glared at me in a cold, hard way. I again felt a surge of animosity towards her. I thought that I was being so sincere and concerned and that she was unfeeling for my discomfort.

She apparently detected my mood, looking away suddenly.

After a long silence I told her that her reaction to me had seemed unfair because I was seriously trying to understand what the blending of energies was about.

"There is nothing to understand," she replied without expression.

I reviewed for her the sequence of unusual events that had taken place since I had met her, starting with how she had assumed her right to a ride to the ranch with me the day I had arrived, and concluding with my feeling that a mysterious energy flow from her was literally changing my life.

She listened in silence.

"What is your interest in me?" I asked. There was no belligerence in my question. I was only curious as to why she felt she had to associate with me.

"You indicated to me that you wanted to know about your Uncle Farley and the ranch," she said.

I noticed a tinge of sarcasm in her voice, as if she were humoring me.

"But what you have shown me has nothing to do with my Uncle Farley and little has to do with the ranch," I protested.

Her reply was that everything had to do with my Uncle Farley and the ranch if I would only open myself to the idea.

I knew it was useless to argue with her. I realized then the total idiocy of my resolution to write my book in a place that was totally foreign to me. I had become fascinated by Alana and whenever I was apart from her I promised myself that I was never going to lose my temper or feel annoyed with her. In actuality, however, the minute she rebuffed me I had another attack of peevishness. I felt there was no way for me to interact with her and that angered me.

"I can't teach you, Heather," Alana said suddenly. "It has all been a big mistake. You already know everything you wish to know and so there is no point aggravating yourself about it. Besides I can't get any more involved with you and your dangerous anger."

I stared at her in disbelief. "What are you talking about?" I asked. I was certain that she had inwardly heard me arguing within myself but was determined not to admit it.

"Just what I said. You don't need me. You have all the answers you want," she said.

"Alana, you know that's not true. I want to learn from you," I said defensively.

"You say you do, but your words and your actions say you

don't," she said.

"That's not true," I said again, suddenly panicked that she was going to leave and I would not see her again.

"It takes too much out of me and you," she said. "Our energies do not blend, they work against each other. I thought it could be different, but now I know."

"But we do blend together," I said anxiously.

She shook her head. We stared at each other for a long moment.

"Alana," I said, "I want to learn from you. Something is happening in my life that I can't explain, but I know it's important. There is something in me that is opening up, a state of consciousness that is developing that I have been hungry for all my life."

She had lowered her eyes when I had started to speak, but she now raised them and looked up at me. Her eyes were fathomless pools, and for a moment I became lost in them.

"Please, let us continue," I begged.

She was slow in answering. "If we were to go on you would have to give yourself to me," she said, "and I don't believe you could do that."

"Yes, I could," I answered. A peculiar feeling settled somewhere inside, a feeling of connection to Alana, as though an intravenous tube was instantly implanted in me to join me to her and connect our life flows. It was as if I was no longer solely myself but myself and her as well, and while making the commitment frightened me, it seemed the only thing I could do. A part of me wanted to run away, and still another part knew that there was nowhere to go but forward.

"Do you want to know why your little adventure today missed the point?" she asked.

I knew she was referring to my experience with the medicine

stones.

"Yes," I answered. The fact that I did not argue or jump to my defense made it clear to me that I had become her student.

"You live too much in the other worlds," Alana said staring at me. "Your life is a fantasy." She hesitated, studying me.

I wanted to argue that it wasn't true, that while I enjoyed simple adventures like the ones I had experienced with the rocks and the medicine wheel, I was in no way divorced from the real world. Instead I kept my mouth shut.

"Do you understand what I am saying?" she asked, glaring at me.

"I think so," I lied.

"Heather, you must learn to live in the now, in this moment, to act in it. Do you understand me?"

"Yes," I answered.

"Good. Now tell me about your book. How far along are you?"

"Just a few chapters," I answered simply. I had made it a practice never to discuss a work in progress with anyone, and her question surprised me.

"Tell me about it," Alana said.

I hesitated. "I can't," I said.

"Why is that?"

I explained the reason and poked fun at myself for it, then asked that she understand my situation. "I've learned," I said, "that when I talk about my work, I never finish it."

Alana smiled and then began humming an unusual tune.

"When a person decides to do something it is important for them to go all the way," she said, "but she must take responsibility for what she does. No matter what she does, she must first know why she is doing it, and then continue without doubt or remorse about it."

She stood, quietly examining me. I did not know what to say. Finally I said, almost in agreement, "I have always felt that way about life."

"But have you always lived it that way?" she asked firmly.

"I think I have," I answered with conviction.

Her eyes held me and for a moment I seemed not even to breathe.

"Tell me, Heather," she said, "why do you write books?"

"Because I love to write," I said quickly.

"And," she prompted.

I hesitated uneasily. "Writing is my tool for self-discovery," I said finally. "That's why I wrote a book with that title."

"You write for yourself, then," she said.

"Yes, of course."

"It's not a good enough reason," she said.

I didn't know what to say. It was the reason I had given my students to write. Why wasn't it good enough for me?

"It's all right for unpublished writers to write for themselves, but as a well-known author you have a greater responsibility," she said. "You must write for the reader. You must want to communicate with the reader, to guide and illuminate."

I was amazed at her command of the English language and by her ability to grasp the heart of a concept. I held the same idea when I first began writing, and found I had to give it up. Writing for a reader made the beginning writer self-conscious. But she was right, I was no longer a beginning writer.

I still did not understand how one could focus on the reader and write fiction as well, and I expressed this concern to her.

"Look at me," she said. "I have no difficulty in being myself and relating to you at the same time. The simplest thing I do is a form of communication: to take you for a walk in the hills may very well spell an adventure. Adventure, or fiction as you call it, is stalking me all the time. Therefore, I become conscious of life and whoever is with me becomes conscious of it too."

I was confused, and said that I didn't understand how one's personal adventure could be called fiction.

"If you are confused it is because you are thinking about it too much," Alana said. "Wasn't it an adventure you had with the magnet stones a little while ago?"

"Yes," I answered, unsure of where she was headed.

"Wasn't the incident fiction as well?" Alana asked.

I suddenly understood what she was driving at, how I had imagined that she had placed the magnet stones in the four corners of the medicine circle and gained an experience from it. I was still confused as to how this related to the reader of fiction.

"The writer presents the adventure, the individual reader turns it into fiction," she said. "Fiction is an excitement of the imagination, an interpretation of the adventure. You must only write the adventure and allow readers to read their own fiction into it."

I could see what she meant, although I had never looked at it that way. Her unusual viewpoint fascinated me. She had a way of saying things that shifted my center of awareness.

"When you write your book, write it as an adventure," Alana said again. "Keep the fiction out of it. Allow the readers to supply that and they will applaud you for it."

"But what about make-believe names and places," I asked, trying to be sure that I understood.

"That kind of fiction is all right for you to write but that is not the fiction we are speaking of," she said. "It's important for you as an author not to get caught up in personal fantasy. Write for the reader and not yourself. Don't be so self-indulgent."

Her ideas were shattering me. I wondered if I was going to have to throw out the work I had done on my book and start all over again. I asked her opinion.

"What does it matter?" she asked cooly. "It is important to make things as correct as one can, it doesn't matter how long it takes to make them correct."

"But I have a deadline," I complained.

She glared at me and I wished that I had kept quiet.

"To assume responsibility for one's work is the important thing," I said quickly, correcting myself.

"It doesn't matter about what is the most important thing," she contradicted. "What matters is that the *do* is correct. If you aren't going to present your book to the reader in the right way, Heather, there is no point in finishing it."

I lowered my eyes in contempt. I wanted to tell her to mind her own business and to stay out of that area of my life, but I knew that to do so would mean that she would leave and I would never see her again.

"The trouble with you, Heather," she said, "is that you don't like to be told what to do. You're all concerned with who's boss, with pecking order."

CHAPTER SIX

WALKING IN COMPANION ENERGY

I slipped through the passageway into the hollow, where I found Alana in the midst of the grazing horses, wrapping the front leg of a chestnut mare. Careful not to make a sound, I sat on the ground to wait. The grey stallion turned his head to look at me and then continued to graze. He was even more beautiful than I had remembered him. His sensitive face looked Arabian rather than mustang and I wondered if he was a domestic horse set free.

Alana finished wrapping the mare's leg and walked silently toward me.

I remained seated so as not to disturb the horses. She sat down next to me.

"What's wrong with the mare's leg?" I asked.

"A nasty contusion," she said, "but the compress of bay leaves should take care of it." She paused, looking deeply into me. "Why have you come?"

I shrugged my shoulders slightly, thinking of what to say. I didn't have any reason, really. I simply wanted to be near her, to watch her, to talk with her and I hoped, learn something at the same time. I was used to feeling filled with her, and every time I worked on my book I emptied part of her out of me and was left feeling lonely, and so I sought her out to fill myself again. "May I stay and watch?" I asked humbly. "I won't get in the way."

She didn't answer for what seemed a long time. "No, Heather, you'll have to leave," she answered finally.

I didn't think that I had heard her correctly and didn't say anything.

"I said you'll have to leave, Heather," Alana said again.

What did she mean I would have to leave? I was so surprised I could think of nothing to say.

"Did you hear me, Heather?"

I was furious and quickly rose to my feet. Who did she think she was talking to? I owned the land. I could stay there if I liked and there was nothing she could do about it.

Alana rose to her feet as well, and before I could say what I was feeling, she turned and began walking back to the horses. I wanted to shout at her angrily, but I managed to hold my tongue. I nearly ran from the hollow back through the passageway.

I was in agony as I ran down the hill through the tall meadow grass. My pride was sorely offended and made part of me lash out at her in hideous anger, while another part understood why she had sent me away.

When I reached the house I hurried inside and slammed the

door. I could barely contain myself and stood with my back to the door, shaking with anger. I knew she had sent me away because of my anger and I hated myself as well as her for it. She had said I had been overly concerned with pecking order, with who was boss, and it was true. I was a celebrity of sorts and used to being in charge of what took place in my life and those who came into it. Alana would not play it my way. Instead she disciplined me by sending me away and I knew that if I defied her our relationship would end.

In a way I didn't care. That is, I could pick up and live as before, or try to do so. Or I could begin anew, but how? I doubted that I could forget Alana and I would never forget the angry part of me that she had exposed. I had never before known that I was an angry person and it appalled me. Before my association with her I had believed myself to be highly evolved in consciousness. I was known among my friends and readers as a very spiritual woman, bold and adventuresome, in tune with nature and destiny.

Several days later Alana stopped by the house and asked me to join her in the hollow where she wanted to show me something. I had prepared myself to resist her, but when I looked into her eyes I could not contain my joy. I had missed her, and her presence uplifted me like the wind beneath the wings of a bird. There was no doubt that I wanted to learn much from her, and I knew that if I had to totally give myself over to her, I would have to find a way to do it.

"Are you over your fit?" Alana asked suddenly, studying me.

Her question struck me funny and I laughed. "Yes," I answered. "I've been writing about it for the past several days and so I'm over it. I feel so exposed," I added pathetically.

She chuckled softly, then said she was glad I had recuperated, and suggested that I pack up a light lunch to take with us.

As we walked up the hill through the meadow she asked me to practice my soft vision, focusing my attention between my eyes in the center of my forehead and remaining aware of any feelings or experiences that came to me.

I tried to follow her instructions, and it seemed that the more focused I was and kept my attention between my eyes, the more I became a part of the environment. That is, I moved through it in an instinctive way, like an animal, rather than with my usual objectivity.

When we reached the passageway into the hollow, we stopped. Alana turned to me. "What was it like?" she asked.

I explained to her what I had felt.

"That is good," she said. "And what did you think about?"

I was silent an unusually long time in an effort to recall what thoughts I had had while coming up the hill. "I don't recall any special thoughts," I said, suddenly excited to discover that while I had walked up the hill I had been inwardly silent, which meant that I had functioned from consciousness rather than thought. I told Alana about my realization.

She smiled knowingly. "Today I want to talk to you about walking in companion energy," she said. Then she told me to continue in soft vision as we entered into the hollow and to maintain that way of seeing for as long as I could. "When it slips away from you," she said, "pull it back. It is in this way that you will remain in a state of heightened awareness."

I was excited and had momentary difficulty in engaging my soft vision until I finally managed to relax again. As Alana went through the passageway I followed her. Once inside the hollow she faced me again.

"When you look at me to listen to me speak, remember to see me with your soft vision," she said, "and when you listen, listen in an easy, soft listening way." She fell silent, studying me.

While looking at her, the focus of my vision diffused about her face, I became aware that her voice both dominated my perception and freed it. I was also fully aware of every sound in the environment as well as every sight. I knew that although she was studying me, she was also viewing the environment from her peripheral senses.

"Walking in companion energy," she said, "means to be in agreement with the world around you. The world does not decide who you are and you do not decide what the world is. When there is an acceptance between the two, there is companion energy."

For an instant I understood, and then I suddenly became filled with questions. "How can the world come to an agreement?" I asked.

She did not answer.

"The world doesn't have a mind in which to question," I said again, "and so that statement doesn't make sense." I started to continue the argument and then realized that the part of me that was arguing was my mind. Alana had asked me to remain in soft vision, which was a condition of consciousness rather than the mental rambling of thought. I suddenly realized that questions came from the realm of thought, whereas acceptance was born in a state of consciousness.

Alana smiled as though she had heard my inner machinery, had watched it go from soft vision to hard focus and back to soft vision again.

"When you live in soft vision, when the agreement between you and the world exists," she said, "you are happy and content. There can be no argument with anyone or anything."

"And there can be no anger," I said with a sense of relief. The discovery of my anger had been a great source of worry to me.

"All negative emotions come from hard seeing," Alana said. "Soft seeing makes only positive emotions."

"But sometimes things happen," I said, "and it makes us see things in a hard way."

"Hard vision is not bad," Alana said, "it is a very useful tool, but we must use it consciously and not become addicted to it as a way of seeing. Sometimes we need to study the head of a pin, but after we finish looking at the pin head we relax again into soft vision."

"You mean that when something happens to make me angry, I can let go of it by shifting my attention?" I asked, aware that I had both asked and answered my own question and had gone from hard to soft vision in the resolution of it.

"Do as I do," Alana said, looking into the hollow. She continued to turn her body in a circle. "As I turn, I shift my attention. Because of what I see here," she paused and then moved again, "I cannot feel the same here. Our feelings are controlled by attention," she said and stopped to look at me again. "If we shift our attention in a hard focus way from one subject to another, we are flip-flopping our emotions, but if we relax our focus and see softly we diffuse them. Soft vision does not disguise anger, it dissolves it. But first you must develop strong enough soft vision to be able to shift your attention from the hard."

We walked on to the far end of the hollow where I had never been before, and Alana took a sharp right. Ahead was a huge Ponderosa forest, and I gasped with delight.

Alana paused and turned to look at me.

"More than anything, I love trees," I said, gazing into the thick forest. A trail wound through it and I was anxious to hurry on.

I reached out to touch the trees as we walked between them. It had been some time since I had seen the puzzle bark of the

Ponderosa and I pointed it out to Alana, telling her that the stand of Ponderosa where I used to live in Oak Creek Canyon was supposed to be the largest in the world. One tree in my yard was 250 feet high and 16 feet around.

After a moment I realized that Alana had not said anything and I fell silent. It was difficult to contain my excitement about the trees, and yet I knew that I was no longer functioning in soft vision. Suddenly I felt resentful. "I don't see anything negative about feeling for trees," I said.

Alana stopped and turned to face me.

"You are always up or down. Companion energy with anything is to accept where you are and who you are with without highs or lows in feeling," Alana said. "To be one with the forest is to have no opinion about it one way or another."

I told her that I wasn't sure I wanted to be feelingless about something that I loved and that I felt that the idea of companion energy should mean that the forest was like a friend to me. As with all friends we express opinions to each other.

"Oh, and what opinion did the forest express to you?" Alana asked sarcastically.

I was irritated by the way she spoke down to me but I caught myself and suddenly looked away, managing to diffuse my vision of the forest. Feeling certain that I had returned to soft vision, I looked at Alana again. "I'm okay," I said confidently. "Sorry for the interruption."

She smiled and softly clapped her hands, then turned and continued to lead the way through the forest.

We came to an S shaped clearing of several acres with a pond or water hole. Alana sat down and motioned me to sit across from her.

"We are going to deal with truths today," she said, looking

wistfully into space and then at me. "I am not Indian and, although I never said that I was, you believed that I was and since I knew that, the lie is mine."

I stared at her totally surprised, too astounded to speak. Her features were Indian, and she not only looked Indian, she acted Indian.

"I apologize to you," she continued. "The clothes I wear are kin to me because they keep me in comfort; they are Indian-like. My principles are also Indian-like but I am a fake." She paused to study me. "I do not know the way of the Indians or their place, although I walk in the same fellowship and family. We share companionship through appreciation."

"I don't believe you," I said skeptically, scrutinizing the very definitely Indian form in front of me. Her high cheekbones, dark skin, and penetratingly deep eyes, even though they were blue, seemed unquestioningly native American. I felt she might be setting me up to trick me in some way and yet she seemed sincere.

"Does it matter, Heather?" she asked.

I didn't know what to say. It mattered because I had believed it, and yet it didn't matter. She had never said that she was Indian; I had assumed it. Whether she was Indian or not had nothing to do with our relationship and the ideas she had shared with me.

I heard the whine of an animal and was momentarily drawn to its sound. Alana did not seem to notice.

"There are those who believe the American Indians to be wise merely because of their heritage. Do you feel that way too, Heather?" she asked.

"No, of course not," I said with conviction. "There are individuals in the native American culture just as in our own."

"If you think that way, can you accept me as a non-Indian guru?" she asked.

I was uncomfortable with her usage of the word "guru" and hesitated. Although I knew that the term merely meant "teacher," to me it smacked of cultism and implied that one person always dominated the other.

"Alana, I don't want a guru at all," I said. The back of my throat constricted and I was unable to finish expressing my thought.

"You don't want a teacher?" she asked, calmly studying me.

I wanted to say no, that instead of a teacher I wanted a friend, a peer, with whom to share ideas. It was true that she had much to teach me but I was sure that I had much to share as well, although she never listened to me, not really. I was familiar with much of what we discussed, but her perspective was new and it shed light in dark areas within me. I knew that within me there were areas of light that could also be shared. Why was I afraid to tell her what I felt?

Alana rose to her feet and walked to the edge of the pond where she stood staring into the water.

From where I sat I could see her reflection in the surface of the water amid the reflection of trees and sky, and I became panicky, afraid that she was going to leave me. Why did I care so much?

She turned to face me.

"I am a Shaman, Heather," she said, gazing at me expressionlessly, "and because of my work, I am only myself, an island walking in companion energy. I belong to no group, no culture, I walk in freedom and I give freely, without expectations of any kind, to whatever and whoever will accept my gifts of healing and personal power."

I wanted to believe her, but the fact that I cared so much for her frightened me. I wondered whether she controlled me somehow by toying with my feelings and attaching them to herself. Once before I had asked her what her interest was in me, why she bothered with me only to be critical of me, and now I asked her again.

"There are many reasons," she said slowly. "You are heir to your uncle's property and your uncle asked me to help you."

"Why would I need your help?" I interrupted, wondering if she was interested in me because I was heir to the property that she wished to own.

"Because, while you are a wise woman among your peers, there are parts of you that are not yet free," Alana said. "You know everything really, but you have not been free to express what you know." She looked at me for a moment, and then bent to the ground to pick up a stick and began peeling the bark from it.

I was astounded by what she said and forgot my fear about her wanting my property. I mulled over the idea that I was not truly free, had never been free, and had accepted a lack of true freedom as a human way of life. How could anyone be truly free in the world and express that freedom in one's daily life? While I had always desired freedom, I had never experienced it.

"Was my uncle free?" I asked.

Alana looked up from the stick she was peeling. "Yes," she said. "He was free, although not always."

"What do you mean?"

"Freedom has to be earned," she said, "there came a time when he earned his freedom and he lived it."

"In what way?"

"In every way," she answered. "Once freedom is won, it is universal within one's life."

"How does one win freedom?" I asked, crossing my arms about my knees as I looked up at her.

"By listening to one's true self, the inner voice, and acting in accordance with it," she said. "But first one must acknowledge the parts of oneself that block freedom, otherwise what we believe to be the inner voice is merely the chattering of our shortcomings speaking to us." She pulled a long fiber of bark from the stick she was holding and dropped it to the ground in front of her. "You, Heather, are the most angry person I ever met. In order to free yourself from that anger, you must look at it."

Again I was appalled that she believed me to be so angry. It was true that I had seen instances of anger in myself since being on the ranch, and I recognized those instances as behavior patterns in myself, but never before had I recognized that I was basically an angry person. I still couldn't accept it.

"My mother tells me I was a very easy child to rear," I said defensively.

"Perhaps that is the root of the problem," Alana said, peeling a second strip of bark and letting it fall to the ground before her. "Perhaps you walked around feeling your mouth taped shut."

I wanted to say that I felt my mouth taped shut now; that it seemed that every word I spoke to her came back to bite me, but I managed to hold my tongue. In silence, I became aware for the first time in my life that I might have to accept defeat. I might have to accept myself as unable to become spiritually adept. In Alana's presence I felt stupid, which meant to me that I must be so.

"It seems the issue you must deal with now is commitment," Alana said, as if responding to my thoughts. "You must decide to accept me as your guru, or not to accept me."

I knew that what she said was true, but I was afraid that if I trusted her, I would lose my identity. I finally told her that.

"Is there some reason you wish to maintain an identity with anger and ignorance?" she asked.

I lowered my eyes, aware of the trickiness of her words. Of course I didn't want to identify with anger and ignorance but I didn't want to be possessed either, not by her or by anyone. I wanted to be my own person. "Alana, the light in which you see me is not the light in which others see me," I said finally. "I am respected in the spiritual community at large."

"That is because you have convinced yourself and others of your spirituality," she said. "It is not because you are spiritually minded."

I was disheartened and wanted to leave and yet deep within myself I knew that I was changing, that a part of me was shifting in viewpoint and expanding in consciousness because of my association with Alana. I felt drawn to continue in that direction. "All right," I said with great effort, "I accept you as my guru."

She didn't say anything but sat back down on the ground in front of me and began to wrap leaves around the stick she had peeled. Then she told me to gather some moss, pine cones, and leaves from around the trees just inside the forest and to bring them to her, which I did. I also found what I believed to be a large hawk feather and gave that to her as well. She then asked me to sit down and be still. I watched her work with the things I had brought her, using strips of pampas grass to tie the moss and leaves to the sticks. When she had finished, to my amazement, she had made what appeared to be a howling coyote.

She handed me the woodland sculpture. "This is for you," she said, "a coyote."

I had been right.

"Coyote is called the trickster because he is master of illusion," she said. "You must begin to be aware of his influence in your life."

I turned the object around in my hand to study it. There was a very definite look to the coyote and its identity was plain to see. I was pleased to receive it from her.

"As your guru," she said, "I will constantly be giving to you. It is important that you give back to me constantly as well."

I didn't know what to say and I was sure that the confusion showed on my face.

"You will find ways to give back to me," she said, studying me. "It's nothing to worry about. " She rose to her feet. I stood up next to her, the coyote in my hand.

"Do you remember earlier at the house that I told you I wanted to show you something?" she asked.

"Yes," I responded.

"It is time," she said.

CHAPTER SEVEN

CHANNELING ENERGIES

Alana led me out of the S-shaped clearing and between a band of trees to another clearing where seven mares, each with a foal, were grazing. One mare in the foreground, a deep bay, raised her head to look at us.

"This is the nursery," Alana said in a quiet voice. "The bay watching us is the lead broodmare." She motioned to the bay. "It is her job to take charge of the others. If she felt them in danger she would send them running on their way but, as you can see she knows me." She then told me to remain where I was.

Alana approached the mare in a slow, easy manner, walked straight up to her, ran her hand down the length of the mare's nose, and then turned and walked slowly back to me.

"You can come in now," she said. She led me some twenty or thirty paces to the center of the clearing. All around us were other mares and their young. One chestnut foal began to run toward us but was distracted by a large white colt who nipped him then reared up on his hind legs to continue the playful attack.

"The white yearling is what I brought you here to see," Alana said. "He is in the weaning stage and is out of sorts with the others. As you can see, he is a nuisance to the other young and their mares and has not yet made the transition to be an adult with the herd."

"Why is that?" I interrupted.

"It is only a matter of time," Alana answered. "Soon his instincts will call him to follow the stallions, unless..." She hesitated and turned to me. "I thought perhaps you would like to have a horse," she said.

I was surprised and thrilled. Since childhood I had wanted to learn to ride and to have my own horse, and now I owned land that was filled with horses and had someone who knew how to teach me about them as well. "I would!" I said enthusiastically. "I would really love to have him."

Alana smiled and then looked at me with a serious expression. "You must do exactly as I tell you," she said.

I nodded.

"When we are with the horses and I tell you something," she said, "you must do exactly as I tell you without argument, and do it quickly."

"I will," I answered, uncomfortable at being spoken to as though I were a child, but anxious to learn.

"Stand right where you are," she said, "and if I tell you to get out of the way, do it quickly, without hesitation."

"Okay."

The white colt paused in his play and turned to look as Alana moved confidently but slowly toward him. The closer she got the more intense he became. His neck arched, his head was held high, and he excitedly snorted as she neared. Every muscle in his body tensed when she stood directly in front of him, slowly raised her hand, and ran it down the length of his nose.

I remembered the gesture as a way of saying hello and remained perfectly still as I had been told.

Next she moved to the side of the colt, holding out her arms, her right shoulder moving slightly in dance-like motion toward his hind quarters, urging him to move from the spot. He pranced away and looked at her from new ground. After a moment Alana advanced toward him, urging him to move with her body language. He quickly pranced in a circle and tried to return to his original place, but Alana beat him to it.

"It is important not to allow him to return to the first piece of ground I took from him," Alana explained softly. "It is the way to establish dominance over him, to advance above him in the pecking order. Do you understand?" She waited for a response from me.

"Yes."

She maneuvered the colt a few more times and then spoke to me again. "Now that he knows that I am aggressive and mean business, I have to remind him that I am also friendly." She walked away from him and then turned and approached him head on, saying hello again by running her hand down the length of his nose. He relaxed and stood perfectly still while she moved to his shoulder and stood next to him, facing in the same direction. With a swoop of her shoulders she stepped forward, and the colt walked with her. She made a wide circle with him and then paused to pat him on the neck. "Good boy."

I was amazed at the naturalness of her movements, by how easily she trained the colt to respond to her. In a quiet voice, I said so.

"I am communicating with him in a language he already knows," she said.

I wanted to ask how she knew horse language but she anticipated my question.

"I lived with these wild horses for many years," she said, running her hand down the white colt's neck. He snorted contentedly and relaxed, lowering his head to graze at her feet. "I observed the manner in which they communicate with each other. With understanding and practice, I gradually worked my way up the pecking order." She straightened her back and the colt raised his head. Then she walked him, turning here and there until he followed her with ease.

"Stay close but not too close," she called out to me.

I wasn't sure what she was going to do and I waited to see.

She remained close to the colt's left shoulder and walked him away from the other horses, then paused to gently pat him on the neck for his good behavior.

"You're amazing, Alana," I said, watching her.

She smiled. "It is all a matter of channeling energies," she said. "Now we'll lead him back to the paddock behind your house so that we can train him and teach you horsemanship."

We walked toward the house, the long way around, so as not to have to lead the horse through the forest. As we walked, Alana told me that the horse was a symbol of power and strength and that in early history only a Shaman was permitted to ride one. "To have a horse of your own," Alana explained, "means that you have taken into your possession both power and strength. How you treat your horse is what you do with your power and strength."

I remained silent for a moment, remembering her earlier discussion of channeling energies, and thought of how little I knew about the subject. The New Age movement used the term in a broad sense, to mean drawing upon the energies of an entity from the spirit realm. I knew that was not what Alana meant. I asked her to elaborate.

Alana suddenly straightened her back and stopped walking. The white colt, who had been walking shoulder to shoulder with her, stopped as well. "Did you see what I did?" she asked.

I said I wasn't sure.

She lowered her shoulders and took a few steps forward. The foal went with her. She raised her back and stopped again, and the foal also stopped. "Did you see?" she asked.

Although I had seen her perform the movement before, until now I hadn't realized that her movements communicated behavior to the foal.

"Body language channels energy," Alana said, gazing at me.

The foal also seemed to be looking at me, and I smiled.

"You are not paying attention, Heather," Alana said, glaring at me.

"Yes I am," I said. "It just seemed that the foal was looking at me because you were."

She continued to glare at me and I suddenly realized that it was true, the foal was looking at me because she was, that he was responding to her channeled energies, to her body language. He mimicked it. I described my realization.

"That is correct," she said, showing neither pleasure nor displeasure. "One way that an individual channels energies is through body language."

"Most people believe that energy comes from outside of themselves," I said. "Your theory turns everything around."

She continued to walk, the foal and me at her side. I realized that both the colt and I were responding to her channeled energy, her forward movement.

"Energy often does come from outside an individual. A conscious person knows how to draw energy from the forces around her; an unconscious person is a victim of it. We channel energy through the body." She fell silent and then added, "It is not my theory that body language channels energy, but Shaman knowledge."

I asked her to explain the difference between body language as a means of channeling energies and "channeling," which refers to tapping into the consciousness of a higher being.

"What do you think it means?" she asked, turning her head to look at me with narrowed eyes.

I accidentally kicked a stone and I stumbled. I said that I wasn't sure and that was why I was asking her.

"I think you are only saying you are unsure," she said, leading the colt forward.

"Perhaps that's true, Alana," I said sincerely, "but it's an area I never felt quite clear on. There's been so much mystique about 'channeling,' about great Beings speaking to us from another realm, that I don't know what to think."

She was quiet for an unusually long time. Finally she said that we would talk about it later. Pointing to my house in the distance, she told me to hurry ahead to fill the water trough in the corral and add some grain to the bin next to it, adding that I would find what I needed in the shed behind the house.

I did as I was told and later, when Alana arrived and secured the foal in the pen, I asked her again if we could talk about channeling.

She leaned against the railing, watching the colt as he explored the area and then settled into eating the grain I had put out for him. "When you look into this pen, what do you feel?" she asked without looking at me.

I was unsure and didn't know what to say.

"I'm asking you to see with your feelings," she said.

I still didn't know what to say, and asked her to be more specific.

"What do your senses tell you happened in this pen before?" she asked.

I gazed past the colt to the far end of the corral, using my soft eye vision to look at the entire area. An image of my uncle Farley came to mind and I imagined him and Alana tending some wounded animals in the corral. I told her what I had seen.

She grimaced and looked away.

I had the feeling that what I had imagined had indeed happened, and I waited for her to tell me about it. But instead of saying anything, she asked me to tell her what else I saw.

Gazing into the pen I envisioned images of wild animals— deer, elk, antelope, and even smaller animals, such as fox and lynx. I turned my attention to Alana and told her what I perceived.

She looked at me a long time before speaking. "Do you get my point?" she asked.

Again I was unsure. I didn't get the connection between what I had seen and her question. Gradually it came to me that she was referring to "channeling," and I asked her if in some way, I had been "channeling" the information I had gotten.

"Channeling comes as a result of perceiving energy, of soft seeing," she explained, while not looking directly at me. "When images strike one's consciousness during soft seeing, there is a state of heightened awareness, and the information given is a form of perception rather than guesswork or thoughtwork."

I asked her if a person's perception was sometimes a result of an entity outside of oneself, but she changed the subject.

"Lying fills holes," she said. "Sometimes when a person lies she is able to create a condition of healing within herself. Some call it cheating, but some cheating is okay." She paused to let me to catch up with her. "Have you played the shell game, where you have to guess which half-shell the pebble is under?"

I said that I had played the game with half walnut shells when I was a child.

"Did you ever cheat?" she asked.

"No, I don't think so," I said, hesitating, "I wouldn't know how to cheat at the game."

"I used to place a hair under the shell that contained the stone," Alana said. "After awhile, I didn't need to cheat anymore, I didn't need the hair under the shell anymore."

"You mean cheating at the game developed your extrasensory perception?" I asked.

"Yes."

"That's interesting," I said thoughtfully.

"It works," she said, turning toward the foal as he suddenly began frolicking around in the pen. "What are you going to call him?" she asked.

I watched the yearling entertain himself, running and bucking about the pen. Although his play was mischievous, he seemed to be well-mannered and docile. "I know what I'd like to call him," I suddenly said.

"What?"

"If you wouldn't mind," I said embarrassed.

She waited for me to continue.

"I'd like to call him Spirit," I said, "because his spirit seems so intact."

"Why not call him Spirit Changer," Alana said expressionlessly, "after me?"

I was pleased. "Okay," I said.

Alana turned on her heels and started toward the house. I ran after her.

"While the colt is settling in," she said, "I'd like to play a game with you." She asked me to scout around on the ground for eleven small, but unusual stones. The stones were to speak to me in some way, and she stressed that I would recognize a speaking stone by my attraction to it. "If you have the urge to pick up a stone," she explained, "it is because there is something between you and the stone, language is being communicated. Respond to it." She told me that when I had collected the stones, I was to wash and dry them and bring them to her on the porch.

Alana sat in one of the two porch chairs and watched me. It took me awhile to find so many special small stones, but I finally did. She gave me an approving glance as I went inside to wash the dirt off the jagged, many colored stones. When I returned I handed them to her. She spread them out on the wooden table between the two chairs.

"The idea," Alana said, looking up from the stones, "is to not pick up the stone I have chosen, not to pick up the one I don't want picked up." She hesitated, studying me. "While playing the game," she continued, "it is important to remember three things."

She waited until she had my strict attention.

"One, is that nothing matters." she said, "Two is that you don't have to understand anything; and three, that there is no competition between us. Do you understand, Heather?"

I said that I was pleased to hear that we were not to compete in playing the game, but that I felt it was important to understand things and that I had trouble accepting the idea that nothing matters.

"For the purpose of my game, you will have to play it my way," she said.

I reluctantly agreed.

"Since I am the one who has chosen the stone not to be picked up, I'll go first," she said. She picked up a stone that was in front of me and then told me to pick up one.

I picked up a stone and waited for her to choose another.

"Your turn," she said after she had drawn another one to her.

I hesitated to shift myself into soft eye vision and then chose another stone.

The game continued until finally there was only one stone left on the table.

"You did a good job," Alana said smiling, "now you pick a stone and I'll see if I can do it." She handed me her stones and I mixed them with mine and then spread them on the table for her to choose.

As I watched Alana pick a stone and remove it, I wondered about the mechanics of what we were doing, but when I asked her, she asked me to wait until we were through playing. After she had successfully not picked up the stone I had chosen, she said that she wanted to choose one more stone and to have me try again. This time I mistakenly picked up her chosen stone on the second try.

"That happens," she said lightly.

"But why?" I asked, wondering what I had done wrong.

"The conscious mind has a way of interfering with the subconscious or intuitive mind," she explained. "It becomes anxious over whether or not you can properly choose again, and then...poof." She paused, indicating an eruption by suddenly opening her hands in front of me. "Anxiety, worry, tension of any kind cuts the flow of our intuition and makes it inoperable. That's why I say don't think too much. The three rules I gave you will teach you how to play: one, it doesn't matter; two, you don't need to understand, and three, the game is not competitive. We will play the stone game often. Gradually your intuitive center will be empowered, and you will be able to use your extrasensory perceptions to communicate with me, with the earth, and everything within it. This type of communication is called walking in companion energy."

I was still not sure I understood what she meant about companion energy, and so I asked her if it had anything to do with "good companion" or "bad companion," as when one person is good for you and another is not good or negative.

She rose from her seat and walked down the porch steps to the corral where the yearling was still nibbling on the grain. I quietly followed her.

"Is the grain that the foal is eating positive or negative?" she asked, turning to face me.

I didn't know what to say and glanced at the foal before looking at her again. "I wouldn't say it is," I said.

"Why not?" she asked.

"It would depend on how the foal reacted to it," I said. The colt looked up at me as though he had heard and understood what I said, and then dropped his head to eat again. "If he liked it, the grain would be nourishing," I said. "If he didn't, well, I suppose there wouldn't be much point to his eating it."

Alana smiled as if to agree and then became serious again. "You mean to tell me that the determining factor in the colt's nourishment is whether he likes or dislikes something?" she asked.

I was confused by her conflicting trend of thought. It seemed she was now pointing to the opposite of what I said, even though at first she seemed to agree with me. I was sure it was true that certainly someone could be nourished by something they didn't much like.

"You were right, Heather," she answered for me, as if she had been listening to my inner discussion, "and you were wrong; that is, both sides of the issue are correct. We can be nourished by something we do not like, but the nourishment is of a lower order and is not then a companion energy. The idea is not to like or dislike anything, but instead to live in acceptance of the energies around us. It is acceptance of an energy that makes it a companion energy."

I stared at her, dumbfounded by her clarity. It was causing a shift deep within the core of me. I felt I was changing right before her eyes. In some inexplicable way she had touched the innermost part of me and I knew I was being transformed. A part of me was dying while another part was being born. I didn't know what to say. I reflected on the fact that she had told me that she was a Shaman and I knew that a Shaman was a healer, but until now I had not considered what that meant.

"Are you channeling your energies to me?" I asked. As I waited for her to answer, I became lost in the depth of her eyes. While looking into them, I saw a tiny image of myself and, for an instant, I felt a sharp pain in my solar plexus. Startled, I looked away.

"...A conscious person knows how to
draw energy from the forces around her;
an unconscious person is a victim of it."

CHAPTER EIGHT
ALIGNING ENERGIES

"**Y**ou asked me if I was channeling my energies to you," Alana said, when she had my full attention. We had been sitting silently on the steps in front of my house playing her stone game and had paused to gaze at the glow of sun setting on the side of the mountains. "Do you still want to know the answer to that question?"

"Yes," I answered, anxious to hear what she would say.

"We are all channeling energies to each other all the time," she said. "The world is a sea of energy and we are submerged in it."

I waited for her to go on but she just sat looking at me as if there was nothing else to say. I wondered whether she was avoiding my question or if she actually believed that she had answered it.

"I can see that you expected me to say something else," she said teasingly. "Perhaps you'd like me to tell you how I used hocus pocus on you to gain your attention."

I knew she was mocking me but I didn't care. "Yes," I answered seriously, "I would like to hear about it." I hoped that she would describe how she used psychic energy to gain my undivided attention. Even though I had no regrets, I felt that I had been manipulated from our very first meeting.

"As I told you before," Alana said patiently, "I do nothing but be myself. If things happen to you it is because you are attracted to the things that happen to you. It means that you are attracted to a story within the sea of energy and you are trying to live it. I am only a vehicle for that which attracts you." She paused to study me. "Does that answer your question?"

"It doesn't explain your influence in my life," I said with certainty.

"You're not paying attention," Alana said, annoyed. Then she rose to her feet and left the porch.

Surprised, I wanted to run after her but I remained seated and watched her walk away.

The next day, when I had finished my morning's work on my book, I went outside and found Alana in the paddock with the colt. I watched her, struck by the fact that she didn't look like herself. For the first time since we had met, she didn't look like an Indian to me. Her dark hair hung loose over her shoulders, falling well below her waist and, instead of the baggy coveralls and colorful shirt that she usually wore, she was dressed in tailored white slacks and white T-shirt. In the center of her shirt was the design of a horse's head. She walked slowly one way and then turned at a right angle, facing me. The yearling was in synchronicity with her, stepping when she stepped and turning when she turned. She brought the horse to a halt and motioned me to her.

I stared at her, unable to believe my eyes. "Alana, you look so different," I said moving closer.

She didn't appear to hear me. "Would you like a lesson?" she asked.

"Yes," I quickly answered.

"Then come inside the paddock," she instructed expressionlessly.

I did as I was told, but instead of going down to the center of the paddock to enter through the gate, I ducked under the rails of the fence.

"There is a gate," she said, as I stood upright facing her, "next time, use it."

I inwardly argued it didn't matter how I entered my own paddock and, when I finally looked at her, I saw that she was glaring at me as if she knew what I had been thinking.

"Did you hear me?" she asked sternly.

I was suddenly so annoyed that I could have yelled at her but instead I looked away. "Yes," I said.

"What did I say?" she persisted.

I struggled for control.

"Heather, I asked you a question, look at me!"

"Why are you picking on me?" I finally snapped.

She continued to glare at me. After a moment she said, "I cannot believe how much abuse I have to take from you."

I wanted to tell her that it was I who was being abused, but I held my tongue.

"I am waiting for you to apologize," Alana said angrily.

"I don't know why you're taunting me this way," I said pathetically. I was trembling in an effort to control myself.

She let out a sigh, the corners of her mouth upturned in a slight smile. "I am doing nothing to you!" she screamed, "you are doing it to yourself!"

A knot tightened in my stomach. I thought I would be sick and wanted to run, but knew that there was nowhere to hide. The deepest part of me was bound to Alana as though an invisible cord connected us, and I felt compelled to be with her. It was my deepest desire to learn what she knew, but I wanted to be treated with respect. I managed to tell her that.

"Respect!" she shrieked. "You want to be treated with respect! You don't even know the meaning of the word."

I thought to myself that she was crazy and it occurred to me that she didn't look like herself today because she wasn't herself. "Is everything all right?" I asked sincerely.

She let out a sigh of exasperation. "Is everything all right?" she repeated. "Heather, what is wrong with you?" She paused, looking deeply into me, and I thought there was genuine concern in her expression. I suddenly felt that the difficulty wasn't coming from her after all, but in some way from me. "Tell me what you think happened here just now," she instructed.

I told her how I felt at being told how to enter the paddock, trying to cover up the fact that I felt that way because it was I who owned the property. I also explained that I responded better to requests rather than demands and that she could speak to me in a kinder tone of voice.

"Ohhhh, like this," she said, mockingly, speaking in a squeaky, childlike voice, mashing her hands together in front of her.

I was annoyed. "Why do you always feel that you have to belittle me?" I asked.

"Because, Heather, you won't wake up!"

"What are you talking about?" I asked.

"If I am your teacher, then you must listen and do as I say," Alana said.

"But to you, I never do or say anything that is right," I said, feeling sorry for myself. "I could say the sky is blue and you would tell me I was wrong, that it is purple."

Alana chuckled. "That's true," she agreed. "and just because I tell you that the sky is purple one day doesn't mean that it won't be blue again the next day. Do you understand, Heather?"

I shook my head, catching a glimpse of the yearling nosing around near the shed at the back of the paddock.

"I am going to try and explain something to you," Alana said.

"All right," I answered.

"Heather, what I am doing with you is trying to align our energies so that you can better receive what I have to give you," Alana said.

"Okay."

"We have talked a little bit about energy, haven't we?"

I nodded, certain that she remembered perfectly well.

"Are you aware that we all have individual energies?" she asked

"Yes," I responded.

No two of us are exactly alike but our energies can be kin to each other," Alana continued. "It is then that the lesser energy extracts power from the stronger energy."

I knew she was referring to our relationship, that I was the lesser energy tapping into her energy, but I didn't understand why she had to be so curt with me and told her so.

"Your feelings get hurt because you believe we have a spiritual bond and because of that bond I shouldn't speak harshly to you." She paused, looking deeply into me.

"Don't we have a spiritual bond?" I asked, feeling badly that she implied it was all my idea.

"You still don't understand bonding and relationships, do you?" she asked.

"I guess not."

"Once a relationship is established, bonding becomes a matter of enhancement," she explained, motioning me to follow her to the back of the paddock where the foal was nibbling at some grass under the fence. She placed a hand on his neck and clucked to him. Spirit turned and stood next to her, shoulder to shoulder. "You see," Alana said, "Spirit and I have established a relationship. Gaining his attention was the beginning of our relationship and the first basic step of successful communication. Next we established the rules of our relationship." She hesitated as though to make sure I was following her trend of thought.

I nodded that I understood. Already I was comparing the relationship with a horse to one with another human being, and I was anxious to hear more.

"We're talking about pecking order," she continued, "about the rules of relationship. Bonding is something entirely different."

"In what way?" I asked, prodding her.

She hesitated thoughtfully. "For example, Heather, you believe you have a bond with me and that the bond with me means that you and I have a rapport. That's true, but our rapport has nothing to do with my remembering to be considerate of your feelings, or vice versa. You are certainly not considerate of mine."

Suddenly aware that what she said was true, I lowered my eyes and raised them again. "I'm sorry," I said apologetically. "I never looked at it that way before."

"That's the trouble with you," Alana said, "you see only yourself in the mirror, no one else."

I couldn't help being annoyed again, feeling that she was taking advantage of my apologetic mood.

"You're looking at yourself again," she said.

I was embarrassed and looked away.

"Stop looking inward so much, look outward to the world around you. Do you understand me, Heather?"

The urge to run away was almost irresistible. I was trembling from head to toe in an effort to maintain composure.

"There is nothing more I can say to you today," Alana said, removing her hand from the colt's neck. She turned and started for the gate, her long hair flowing behind her. With a burst of energy, the colt suddenly darted forward and bucked. As I watched her leave, tears were streaming down my face.

That afternoon I went into town intending to check the mail, fill the Jeep with gas, and set out for Colorado Springs to think things out for a few days. A letter from a publisher changed my mind.

The writer said that the book I was working on had sparked interest at the publishing company and asked me to send what I had finished as soon as possible. I knew that there was no way I would send what I had written, that my story of what I had experienced with Alana exposed me as a spiritual novice. How could I expose myself as the type of individual that Alana had proved me to be? Where was my prowess, my cunning, my adeptness? What would it be like for all the world to know that I was merely an angry person filled with self-pity, and that it was the combination of anger and self-pity that produced the illusion of spirituality that others saw in me. I was humbled by my new self-image and recalled how Alana had told me to stop looking at myself in the mirror and to look outward.

I got in the car thinking that I would head back to the ranch for an objective look at what I had written. Then it occurred to me that Spirit was low on grain, and I pulled over to the feed store.

"How's it goin' out at the Farley place?" the man asked as he loaded the grain into the back of my Jeep.

"Just fine," I answered politely, "it's a beautiful place."

"Should be," the man said, giving me the eye as he brushed off his hands. "Hugh Farley was the richest man in these parts."

I took his comment to mean that my uncle was rich both in resourcefulness and in land, and smiled gratefully at him.

"Didn't Alana ever show you the mine?" he asked.

"What mine?"

"Never really knew what kind of mine it was," the man said, aware that he had aroused my interest. "I only know that your uncle carried bags of ore into the city about once a month."

"How do you know that?" I asked.

"I seen him," the man answered, pausing to motion to the other workers around him, "we all seen him."

"But you never knew what kind of ore it was?"

"Could be gold," the man said.

I tried to dismiss the idea, saying that if there was any kind of mine on the property I would have found it. I closed the back of the Jeep and drove off.

All the way back to the ranch I thought about the implication that Alana knew about a mine and had said nothing to me about it.

When I pulled up in front of the house, I expected to see Alana. I looked in all directions, even checking the back of the house where the foal was corralled, but she was nowhere in sight. I recalled how unusual she had looked the last time we had met and wondered whether she had previously appeared Indian merely to gain my confidence.

Uneasily, I drove the Jeep to the back of the house and unloaded the grain at the side of the shed next to the paddock.. Spirit pranced anxiously in place as I split open the sacks and poured the grain into the bin; then he began to run back and forth.

I watched him, recalling how Alana had tamed him so that I could have a horse, and I thought her method of training seemed easy and natural compared to her treatment of me. In many ways she treated us the same; that is, she demanded total attention and concentration from us both, so insistently that I felt that if I gave in to her I would lose my free will and become possessed by her. Consequently, I always held back and I knew that my refusal to submit to her was the true reason for our disputes.

"I want to be myself!" I shouted defiantly. The colt looked at me as if to ask, "So why all the fuss?" then kicked up his heels and pranced to the other side of the paddock. Watching him, I suddenly felt a sense of confidence in my personal power, and I slipped through the rails of the fence to be inside with him. I wanted to try to work with the colt in the way Alana did, but he bit my right hand before I knew what was happening. I quickly leapt to the safety of the other side. My hand was bleeding and I went into the house to bandage it.

The bite Spirit gave me was extremely painful. Fortunately, I am left-handed so that even though typing was painful, I could still push a pencil and continue working on my book. For the next few days I did not seek out Alana and she did not visit the house. I dreaded having to explain my injury to her, and I was grateful for the time to heal my hand before seeing her again.

One afternoon I pulled a surveyer's map from my file and studied the lay of my land, looking for an area that could contain a mine. I soon realized that a mine could be almost anywhere, disguised by nature. I noticed that on the far side of the hollow, beyond where Alana had taken me to fetch Spirit, the trail wound around to the back of the hillside and disappeared. I decided to explore.

I checked to see that Spirit had ample water and feed and set out. When I reached the hollow, Alana was there working with the horses, and I stopped to watch her. Stony, the big grey, was on his knees bowing to her. It was amazing to see such a great beast so willing to please; I knew I would never forget it. She motioned for him to rise and he did, then she handed him a stick, which he took in his mouth. To my surprise, he began to chase her with it. Alana dodged the stick, running one way and then the other, zigzagging to get out of the horse's way, playing and laughing like a child. Suddenly all of the anger I had felt toward her melted and was replaced by genuine affection.

The horse was the first to see me, he hesitated in his play, and Alana turned abruptly to see what had caught his attention.

"Hello, Alana," I called.

She did not answer but stood looking at me.

I told her that I was looking for a mine I'd heard about from the man in the feed store.

"What did he tell you about the mine?" Alana asked suspiciously.

"He didn't have anything to tell, just that there was one," I answered.

Alana chuckled, and bent over to dust the dirt from her coveralls. Then she patted Stony, telling him he was a good boy, and stepped back from him, crisscrossing her hands and brushing them together, signaling the horse to "go trot." Stony darted away from her and rejoined the grazing herd a few hundred feet away.

"Come on," Alana called, motioning for me to follow her, "I'll show you your Uncle Farley's mine."

As soon as I caught up with her she spotted the bandage on my hand.

"What happened?" she asked.

I told her that I had bumped it against something sharp but she guessed immediately what had happened.

"Did Spirit bite you?" she asked.

"Yes," I said, feeling foolish.

"I told you not to play with that foal until you know how to handle him," she admonished.

I tried not to be annoyed but I was, and quickly looked away.

"I can just imagine how it happened," Alana said mockingly. "You slipped between the rails of the paddock and just as you got to the other side, Spirit bit you."

Surprised, I glanced briefly at her and quickly looked away again.

"Well, is it true?" she asked.

"Yes," I said, not looking at her.

She chuckled again and began walking faster.

"How did you know?" I asked.

"Foals are mouthy creatures," she said, "you must be more careful."

I realized she wasn't going to tell me how she knew I had been bitten because there simply wasn't any way for her to tell me. I had been around Alana long enough to know that when she said she knew something, she knew it through extrasensory perception, which she couldn't explain.

We walked quietly to the back of the hollow, and we were suddenly standing near the mouth of a large cave. I wondered why she had not already shown me the place.

"Go on inside," Alana said.

I stepped inside the cave. The first thing I saw was Alana's drum hanging on the wall and then I saw her other possessions neatly stacked on ledges, and in the center of the cave, a bed. The bed consisted of a large blanket thrown over a tidy pile of leaves and moss. Farther back in the cave were several half-filled ore bags like those described by the man at the feed barn. There was no doubt that I had entered the place where Alana lived.

"What's in the bags?" I asked.

"Go take a look," Alana said.

I moved closer to one of the bags, sat down and pulled open the drawstring at the top. A pungent odor greeted me. Inside were partially crushed leaves and berries and an occasional root. I turned to look questioningly at Alana.

"What is it?" I asked.

"Just what it looks like," she answered, "herbs and roots, medicine I make for those who need it. Your Uncle Farley used to distribute it for me in the community. Perhaps now you'll help me."

I was filled with a new sense of humility and again embarrassed about my suspiciousness. "Are you a medicine woman?" I asked.

"I am a Shaman," she answered. "I told you a Shaman is a healer. There are many ways to heal; one way is through the use of plants."

Noting that Alana had seated herself on her bed, I sat down on the ground where I was. "What other ways are there?" I asked curiously.

"The most important healing," Alana said, "is one that is difficult to describe."

"Is it a psychic healing?" I asked.

"Not from my psyche," she said, "but it employs the psyche of the individual being healed."

"I don't understand."

"Why do you wish to know so much?" Alana asked, eyeing me.

"Because I wish to learn."

"Why?"

I hesitated, reluctant to say out loud something that I had never admitted to myself. "Alana, I'd like to learn to be a Shaman too," I said sincerely.

She stared at me a long while before answering. "You already know everything, Heather. You merely lack the freedom to express it."

"What do you mean, freedom?" I asked. "I live in the world but not of it — how free can a person be?"

A slight smile crossed Alana's face and then disappeared again and I noticed that the light in the cave brightened and dimmed again as well. "The freedom I am speaking of comes to a person who has had her holes filled. Do you know what holes are?"

"No."

"Holes are areas of infection in one's life," she explained. "It is a Shaman's role to clean out the infection and to fill the holes."

"Would you please show me one of my holes?" I asked.

Alana shook her head. "I don't care to take on your abuse," she answered.

"Please, Alana," I pleaded, "I promise you there will be no abuse."

She shook her head again.

"Please!" I pleaded again.

"Do you have your notebook with you?" she asked.

"Yes," I said, withdrawing it from my pack. I thought she would want me to write something down.

"Do you have many notes in it?" she asked.

"Oh, yes," I said, holding the book protectively, "nearly every little, secret thought I've ever had."

"Give it to me," Alana said, reaching out her hand to take my book.

"Oh, no, I couldn't do that," I said, holding onto it tightly.

"Give it to me," Alana said again.

"I can't, Alana! I never show my notebook to anyone."

"You must give it to me," she said.

I knew that she really meant it and I started to panic.

"And so you now see one of your holes," Alana said, withdrawing her hand. "Your secrecy is false, your hiding place a dark hole inside your own mind."

Suddenly I knew what she was talking about. All my life I had tried to hide my feelings from others and my notebook was a physical manifestation of it. I handed her the notebook. "I wish to be a Shaman," I said again, with renewed determination.

She took the notebook from my hand, opened it at random, and began to read silently. I shifted my weight uneasily. She looked up at me with a stern expression. "This is terrible," she said.

I quickly reached for the notebook. "Give it back to me," I said defensively.

She smiled and gave it back.

I realized that she had placed a finger in the infection of my overly sensitive nature and I lowered my eyes.

She didn't say anything.

"I don't want that part of me, that hole any more," I said slowly, lifting my eyes to meet hers.

She smiled. "Recognizing a hole is the first step in filling it," she said.

"I suppose I have other holes," I said.

She nodded her head.

"Are there many?" I asked uneasily.

"Do you know what a colander is?" she asked.

I stared at her in disbelief. "I have that many?" I asked.

"At least they're not all big ones," she said, and smiled.

"Well, thank God for that."

We both laughed.

"Will you help me Alana?" I asked.

She didn't answer.

"I will do as you tell me," I said again.
She still didn't say anything.
"I do want to be a Shaman," I said.
"It takes years," she answered.
"I don't have years," I said, "for me it'll have to be faster."
"That is another one of your holes," she said.

CHAPTER NINE
SUBMISSION

I sat quietly with my head bowed inside Alana's cave, reflecting on the flaws she had pointed out. I understood for the first time why a Shaman was called a healer and what the term healer meant. I was changing in spite of myself. It didn't seem to matter how much I inwardly and outwardly kicked and squirmed or argued, I was becoming refined. The old Heather Hughes-Calero was fading away, becoming obsolete.

"There is something I want to show you," Alana said, breaking into my silence.

I slowly looked up at her, half afraid to learn what it would be.

She went to the other side of the cave where she lifted a slim cloth portfolio and thumbed through the papers inside. Withdrawing one, she returned to sit in front of me. "This is a drawing I did some years ago," she said, showing me the paper.

I looked at the drawing, a face, with immediate recognition.

"Who does it look like?" she asked, watching me.

The hair was darker than my own, but the shape of the face, the eyes and the expression in them, the nose, and the mouth were mine. I was too astounded to speak.

"Well?" she prodded.

I looked at her, her dark-blue eyes were like pools and I remembered my feelings when I first looked into them that fateful day I had found her in my Jeep. Then, as now, gazing into them was like gazing into a reflection of myself, only this time instead of an actual image, I saw a void, a silent no place, no one space where not even thought existed. "It's me," I said humbly.

She nodded.

I wanted to ask how she had come to make the drawing before we met, but the words would not form in my mind.

"Isn't it interesting," she said, "that I made a drawing of you as an adult before you were one."

I remained quiet, looking at her, waiting for her to continue.

"I have known for a very long time that you were to be the student who would crown me," Alana said in a soft voice. I leaned forward. "It is destiny that has joined us, your's and mine. There can be no rush to its goal. There is a lifetime to complete our work; the journey is forever."

In rising panic, I lowered my eyes. How could I tell her that I didn't want to be with her forever, or with anyone else for that matter. I simply wanted to be a free agent, bonded to no one, operating from consciousness or heightened awareness, to live in the world alone, myself an adept and spiritual teacher. I was drawn to learn from her but it was not my intention that our teacher/student relationship would be long-lived. I intended to leave when my book was finished and to come back only in retreat from my busy life within the world. Of course, I hoped that we would always be friends, good friends, but nothing more.

Alana sat watching me as if she was listening to my inner chatter. "Look out of yourself," she said softly, "and then you will not be so frightened."

"I'm not frightened," I said, raising my eyes to meet her's.

"Yes, you are," she said, "you are afraid of close relationships, afraid that they will consume you, and so you are always looking for a way out."

Uneasy, I lowered my eyes. I sat silently a moment and then, without looking at her, I told her what I felt.

"You are looking inside at the little self," she said patiently, "Heather Hughes-Calero the personality is carrying on a conversation with Heather Hughes-Calero the personality." She waited, until I was forced to raise my eyes to meet her's. "When you look inward, the personality confronts the lower self and is met with fear, suspicion, and hostility. Look outward instead, and you are Soul viewing and participating in the pictures of life." She put the drawing to one side and rose up on her knees. "You say you want to be a Shaman," she said.

"Yes," I answered.

"Do you know why?"

I hesitated, trying to formulate an answer she would accept and that would also get me off the hook about remaining her student for years to come.

"I'll tell you why," she said, gazing at me. "Your desire to be a Shaman gives you permission to focus on yourself and that's your true desire, your intent, so you can have a holier-than-thou walk to cover up. This is your greatest hole."

I was appalled. Her words pierced me as if I had stumbled heavily into the thorns of a catsclaw bush. "That's not true," I cried out, protesting that she had been unfair in her assessment of me.

"You've felt holy for so long, you now believe it," she said.

"That's not true!" I shouted.

"There is little about you that is true and it's time you truly recognize yourself," Alana said sternly. "Do you understand me?"

"Yes," I said, giving in so that she would ease up on me.

"No, you don't," she said mercilessly, "you say you do to move away from the subject, but you don't."

Deep down I knew what she said was true, that from an early age, I had adopted a spiritually superior attitude. It had become such a comfortable self image that I had forgotten that my superior feelings originated as a cover-up for inferior ones. I began to cry as I looked at Alana again.

"Heather, I can see now that I was mistaken," she said. "It may have been our destiny to meet, but the relationship I spoke of cannot be, not at this time."

I knew she was pushing me from her and my sense of loss was overwhelming. I began to sob.

"You weep for yourself," Alana said pitilessly, "always yourself. Poor little Heather."

She rose to her feet and told me to leave.

I jumped up and hurried out of the cave, blinded with self-pity as I made my way through the hollow and back down the hillside. When I got to the house I started to pack, telling myself that it was the right time to leave, rationalizing that because the book I had come to write was nearly finished, and the publisher wanted it as soon as possible, I was better off finishing it in the city. I might have gotten away with deceiving myself if I hadn't awakened in the middle of the night in an angry rage.

The rage emerged from the depths of myself, splitting me in two and, for the first time in my life, I understood the meaning of hate. As I thought of Alana and the way she had treated me, a part of me was consumed with hatred for her. Was this the hideous face of

God that the spiritual adepts cautioned their students about, the poisonous flip side of love? In one instant my hate became so intense that I became feverish. Sharp pains dug at my abdomen and I screamed as my body curled and retched on the bed, yet never did I lose awareness of a consciousness in me that watched. The invisible side of myself warned that if I didn't stop hating Alana, I would destroy myself physically, mentally, and spiritually, and I knew there was only one way to stop the poison. I could not leave. I would have to confront myself, my fraudulent self, and beg Alana to take me back.

The next morning I set out to find her. The sky was filled with thick, puffy, white clouds which, when I reached the hollow, had merged and darkened, a sure sign that a storm was brewing. I hurried to her cave and hesitated at the entrance. Looking in, I could see no one.

"Alana," I called softly, "are you in there?"

There was a long silence and then she answered. "Yes, what is it?"

"May I speak with you a moment?" I asked politely, looking into the cave and still not seeing her.

I heard her sigh and, for an instant, I resisted an urge to run away. "Please!" I pleaded.

"What is it, Heather?" she asked, as if invisibly nearby.

I spun on my heels to find Alana standing next to me. She had not been in the cave as I believed but outside, watching me as I called in to her. She waited for me to speak.

My mouth was dry as I told her what I had experienced in the night and my revelation that I had to confront the hole she had shown me in my self.

"Now that you have gotten that off your chest, you are free to leave," she said.

A knot formed in the back of my throat and I glanced away in an effort to control myself before looking at her again. She appeared older somehow, tired, and the lightness that I had witnessed while she was at play with the horses was no longer discernible. "I am so sorry, Alana," I said, "so very sorry."

Alana stared at me and her expression cautioned me. "What are you sorry for?" she asked.

"I am sorry that I hurt you," I said apologetically, "and I am sorry that I have been so difficult to deal with. I will do better. I have to do better. I realize now that I have nowhere to go, nowhere to run, that if I don't make it with you, I won't make it at all. The part of me that is valuable will die and the rest of me will follow in a short time." I paused, then said, "I want to be a Shaman, to be your apprentice, with the intent to be a student forever, connected to the breathing earth for the purpose of sharing with others. I will make every effort to respond with joy to your every request of me."

"And you will never argue with me again," Alana said, studying me.

"I can't say that Alana because I am so conditioned to arguing, but I will try," I answered.

"You will make every effort to do as I say," she said.

"Yes."

"Even if it is not to your liking."

"Yes."

"And you promise you will not rush."

"Yes."

"And you will be happy."

"Yes."

"Heather, does this mean you are submitting to me?" she asked.

"Yes."

She looked at me a long time, as if deciding if I could uphold my agreements with her, then finally said, "All right, we will move forward."

CHAPTER TEN

COMING DOWN OFF THE MOUNTAIN

"**I** am glad you are here to help me," Alana said, handing me two ore bags. "It's a long way into town on foot."

"Alana, you can always count on me," I said matter-of-factly, turning to leave the cave with her.

She paused, gave me a questioning look and then stepped ahead of me. I was embarrassed. Her look reminded me of all the times I had argued with her, as well as all the ugly thoughts I had had about her during those arguments. I wished that I had not spoken.

We stepped outside. The clouds had shifted to the East and a clear sky greeted us overhead. It was mid-afternoon and sunny. The horses grazed in the distance. Stony kept looking our way.

"Things have changed," Alana said, looking first at the sky and then around the hollow. "Can you see how different everything is now?"

"Yes," I answered.

"Tell me what you see," she said.

I explained that while there were still clouds, I saw a change in the weather and its effect on the lighting within the hollow, as well as a calm in the environment that wasn't there before.

"It is a warning," she said, looking first at me and then about the hollow again.

Unsure, I hesitated, studying the concerned expression on Alana's face. "In what way?" I asked finally.

"We must not speak of it," she said, glancing from me to the terrain.

"Why not?" I asked, worried.

She gave me a sharp look and then turned and began to lead me out of the hollow.

"Why can't we talk about it?" I asked her again as I hurried to catch up.

She paused to glare at me and then began to walk hurriedly again. "Be careful of those herbs," she said.

I tightened my grip on the bags of herbs I was carrying and skipped to keep in step with her, wondering if she was trying to capture my attention by setting the stage for a mystery, or if there really was cause for alarm. Once in awhile she would glance up at the sky and I would look up in anticipation, but I kept my questions to myself, feeling more and more childlike in her presence.

When we reached the bottom of the hill, she pointed above and beyond the house to a flash of white light in the sky. "Did you see it?" she asked.

I said that I did, but before I could say anything else she had rushed off toward the house and I hurried behind her. It occurred to me that the white light was a distant lightening flash and that it was going to rain. When we arrived at the house she asked me to get the Jeep and that she would wait for me to bring it around front.

I did as I was told and, when we were finally settled and driving down the road toward town, I asked what all the mystery was about.

"There is no mystery," Alana said patiently, "I merely told you that the change in the environment that we saw in the hollow was a warning. When one receives a warning, one is wise to heed it."

"The warning was the change in the weather," I reiterated, not certain of where her thoughts were headed.

"Yes, but it was a warning for more than the weather," she said.

"I don't understand," I said, shifting my eyes from the road to her and back again. It was quiet outside; no birds or other wildlife could be seen.

"You realize it appears that there is going to be a rainstorm," she said.

"I figured as much," I answered.

"It is not a time when it normally rains," she said distantly, staring up at the sky.

I recalled the rainstorm on the day of my arrival. Several months had passed and it seemed natural to me that it would rain again now. The land was dry and waiting for moisture. I told her what I felt.

"It is not going to rain," Alana said. "I told you that what we have seen is a warning."

I wondered how she could be so sure but knew better than to question her about it. Instead, I asked about something that I had been wanting to understand for a very long time. "Alana, when we first met, you said that there are others living with you on the mountain," I said, "but, except for the illusion in the hollow that day, I have seen no one. Are there others hidden on the mountain?"

"I appreciate your helping me with my work," she said as if she had not heard me. "Many people count on me to help them become well."

I knew she wasn't going to talk about the others and so I asked her to tell me about her work in town, but she declined, telling me that I would see for myself, which was worth more than any explanation she could give.

We rode silently until we came to a small, half mud, half stone house on the outskirts of town. She asked me to pull up there. I made a sharp turn onto the dirt driveway and slowly rolled to a stop in front of the house. A Mexican woman and a young child appeared in the doorway. At first the woman looked at me suspiciously but when she saw Alana she hurried around to the other side of the Jeep to greet her, chattering excitedly in Spanish. Alana listened, answered her in Spanish, and then motioned to me.

The woman nodded respectfully. "You are welcome here," she said in perfect English.

"Thank you," I replied, surprised that she did not have an accent.

The wind had picked up and stirred the brush on the ground as we climbed out of the Jeep and followed her into the house. Alana brought one of the herb bags with her. Inside, the woman started chatting in Spanish again but Alana asked her to speak English so that I could understand what she was saying. The woman hesitated, studying me, and then continued in English.

"Sleep does not come easily these days," she said to Alana, "there are so many uncertainties in life."

"It is good to have uncertainties," Alana said. "One cannot progress without a creative imagination."

The woman turned to straighten the small altar on the cupboard next to her and fidget with a little statue of the Virgin Mary before she looked at us again. "I don't understand you doña Alana," the woman said angrily, "if I let my imagination tell me what to do, I will live in this crummy house forever."

"Then change your imagination," Alana said. "Recreate your world, but not just in your imagination. Do something to make yourself see better with it. As it is, you are always pushing what you want from yourself by looking at what doesn't work. Look at what works, not at what doesn't work." She paused, studying her. "Do you understand me?"

The child pulled on his mother's skirts, pointing toward the window and the stream of black clouds overhead. She motioned him to go to a chair and be still. "I want my son to go to school," she said.

"Then find a way to send him," Alana said.

"We have no car, and he is only a little boy who cannot walk so far to school," the woman said.

Alana silently studied her until she finally looked away. "Do you really want your son to go to school?" Alana asked.

"But of course, I told you," the woman answered, quickly looking at her and then away again.

"Then gather your things. We will take you and your son to town where he can be educated," Alana said.

"But we will have no place to live," the woman protested, looking full at Alana.

"Decide to make your way and you will," Alana said.

"But it's not possible."

"You are a good cook," Alana said, "and you have a love for children."

"That is true," the woman answered.

"Then see yourself cooking and working with the children at school in exchange for a place to live," Alana said.

"But suppose they already have such a person at the school," the woman said.

"Does that mean that you cannot help that person?" Alana asked.

"No, but suppose that person will not want me?"

"Again, I will say to you to imagine ways that work instead of ways that will not work," Alana said.

The woman stared at Alana. Gradually her expression softened. "Doña Alana, I want to believe you, and so I will try," she said.

"That is good," Alana answered, nodding approvingly, "but you must also want to believe yourself."

"Perhaps I should spend time imagining my new life," the woman said. "Every day I will work at it."

"You must work at more than imagining," Alana said, "you must do a thing as well as imagine it."

"Soon," the woman agreed.

Alana smiled as if she understood. "Soon is good," she said, "but now is better."

The woman appeared panicky. "Now?"

Alana nodded. "We have room in the Jeep and Heather will drive you," she said, turning to me for approval.

I nodded that it was okay, although I wasn't convinced that the woman was capable of caring for herself and her child as Alana suggested.

The woman called to her child to gather up a few clothes and possessions while we waited in the Jeep.

The sky was suddenly clear and the air was still; there was no more wind. I reflected on what Alana had said about the change in weather being a warning. I wanted to ask if the warning was over, and about her certainty of the woman's welfare, but I managed to hold my tongue, to observe rather than question. In my spiritual experience, such things were considered possible only after a great deal of inner preparation. If I had advised the woman, I would have suggested a plan of contemplative exercises whereby she could first build up the stamina and confidence to survive in town, and then let people know what she wished to do.

The woman and her child walked quietly to the Jeep, carrying a large cloth bag of personal belongings. I got out and helped them into the narrow back seat and wrestled with the bag until I managed to force it into the remaining space.

No one spoke on the way into town and Alana appeared to be sleeping in the passenger seat.

"Drive up in front of the school," Alana said, opening her eyes as we reached the outskirts of town.

I slowed down and looked around but didn't see a school.

"It is off the next right," she said.

The boy whispered something to his mother in the back seat and she asked him to be quiet.

I turned right at the intersection. An American flag waving from a pole in front of a brick building indicated that we had arrived. I stopped and turned off the motor. Alana got out and raised her seat so the Mexican woman and her boy could get out. They hesitated, obviously nervous, and then stepped out of the Jeep. The woman stood in front of Alana as if expecting her to say something but Alana merely flashed a well-wishing smile and got back in the Jeep. She placed a hand on the steering wheel and patted it, signaling me that it was time to go. I started the motor and slowly drove off, glancing in the rear view mirror to see that the woman and child were still there, looking after us.

"Drive to the post office," Alana said.

I made a sharp turn back onto the main road and a block later pulled into the tiny post office parking lot.

"You come in with me," Alana said, opening her door. She reached to the floor in front of her seat and took one of the ore bags with her. I wondered why she had not left one with the Mexican woman as it seemed she had intended to do, but I knew better than to ask. I got out and followed her inside the building.

"I'm going to get my mail, Alana," I said, sliding my key into the box as she went on through a glass door into the shipping section. In my box were a number of letters, mostly from my readers, but also one from a university and one from my publisher.

Alana watched me through the glass door and then stepped back outside. "Who wrote you?" she asked, eyeing the letters in my hand.

I told her and started to put the mail away in my handbag.

"Better open the one from your publisher," she said.

I was surprised but did what I was told. It was a letter from the vice president of acquisitions, attached to a contract for "Woman Between the Wind." I told her what it was.

"Good, we can use the money," she said.

I was surprised at her use of "we" but said nothing.

"It's time you and I had a contract," she added.

I stared at her and waited for her to continue but she said nothing. "Okay," I said, "since the book is about our experiences together, I think it's right that you receive half of what I earn from it."

She smiled in a way that told me she was pleased, then went through the glass door again. The postmaster greeted her and accepted the bag of herbs she was carrying. There was a moment of intense conversation between the two and then she joined me again. I was reading the letter from the university.

"What's happening?" she asked.

I continued to read and then told her that the letter was reminding me that I was to lecture to philosophy students in a few weeks. The news seemed to please her but she said nothing about it.

"I have one more stop to make," Alana said.

"Okay, where to?" I folded the letter and placed it, along with the others, in my handbag.

"The feed barn, you know where it is?"

"Yes." I remembered the man who had mentioned Alana and the mine on my property.

She started out, then stopped and looked at the postmaster on the other side of the glass door. He looked back at her uneasily, or so it seemed, and moved away from the counter, out of sight.

I followed Alana outside and climbed into the Jeep. "Is the postmaster sick?" I asked.

She seemed to be lost in thought and not to hear me, so I asked her again. "What's wrong with the postmaster?"

"It's always the same," she answered. "Warnings come into people's lives and they refuse to heed them." She turned to look at me from the passenger seat. "A warning is a waking dream. It's the force of life trying to tip us off to something that could cause us trouble, but most people won't listen."

I asked her if she could give me another example of a warning or waking dream.

She turned and looked around the street. "Do you see anything striking? " she asked.

An old man hobbled across the road to a beat up yellow tow truck. He climbed into the cab, rolled down the window, and looked up and down the street as though he expected to see something. "There!" I said, pointing. "He seems to be looking for someone."

"Does he see you?" Alana asked.

"Doesn't seem to."

"Good," she said, "if he had, it could be a warning that you would need his services."

"You mean everyone we look at or speak to is a waking dream warning us," I said.

"I said they could be," she answered.

I stared at her in disbelief.

"The letter from the university was a signal for you to remember that you are to lecture at their institution," she said.

"Yes, I see what you mean," I said thoughtfully.

"But it means more than that," she added.

I looked at her questioningly.

"The mail you just received is a signal that the world is coming in to you," she said. "When you draw people to you it is a sign of personal power. Had you not had any mail, the signs would have read differently."

"Suppose my letters had been merely delayed in the mails?" I asked unbelievingly.

"Then the sign would tell you that you were experiencing delay," she said simply.

I was thoughtful, struck by the clarity of her words.

"There you go again," she said, "you are hopeless."

"Why do you say that?" I asked.

"You're always mulling things over," she answered. "Why can't you accept what I say and leave it alone?"

"I wanted to think about it, Alana," I said, feeling misunderstood.

"To what purpose?" she snapped.

"To make sure I understood you," I whined.

Alana shook her head. "Heather, there are two types of students," she said. "One is an alive student who simply approaches the teacher with 'Here, I am!' The alive student has no preconceived concepts or opinions in the face of her teacher's knowledge."

She looked me full in the face. "And the other student is a dead student, one who is too full to receive from the teacher. The dead student always tries to compare what she thinks she knows with what the teacher says, picking at the gifts that are given. Can you guess what type of student you are, Heather?"

Offended, I lowered my eyes.

"Tell me, are you mulling over what it is like to be dead?" Alana asked cruelly.

I was struck by her implication that I was dead and, though I tried not to show it, an uncontrollable stream of tears slipped down my cheeks.

She chuckled. "I knew you were mulling it over," she said. "Dead students always mull things over, it is what makes them dead."

I wanted to ask her why she felt it necessary to be so cruel to me but I knew the answer. It shocked me to admit the fact that I was a dead student, filled with preconceived notions, concepts, and opinions. I was always comparing and passing judgment on whatever was presented to me and I knew she knew it. After some moments of staring into the empty street I said, "You are the most difficult teacher I have known."

"I am the only real teacher you have ever known," she said matter-of-factly.

I thought I would be sick. A sudden pain swelled in my abdomen and then disappeared as I tried not to cry. I had had many teachers in my life and they were all considerate of my feelings, always encouraging, never discouraging. If I was dead, why did she bother with me? After a few struggling moments, I managed to say what I was feeling without looking at her.

"Isn't it interesting that you are dead and feel it," she said, glaring at me.

I did not look back at her but started the engine and drove into the feed barn parking lot.

"You come with me," Alana said, getting out.

I turned off the motor and stepped outside, trying to focus on the sunlit shine on a tall bush in front of the Jeep. Tears streamed down my cheeks as fast as I could brush them away and then I touched a leaf, held it between my fingers a moment and let it go. The tears stopped. I turned to Alana, who stood with her back to me, waiting for me to compose myself.

"Thank you for waiting," I said.

Without looking back she began walking toward Swede's Western Shop and Feed Barn. I hurried to catch up and walked alongside her.

Outside was a rack of women's clothing. She lifted a pinstriped pant suit from the hanger and stared at it for a long moment.

"Do you like this?" she asked.

"Yes, and it would look lovely on you, Alana."

She glanced at me, then back at the pantsuit, and carried it into the shop.

"Howdy," Swede's wife said from behind the counter.

"Hello, Erma," Alana said politely. "I'd like to try this on."

"Sure," Erma said, motioning toward the dressing room door. "Help yourself."

Alana disappeared and I waited outside, pretending to look through the many racks of clothing. The pain in my abdomen had returned and was growing more and more intense.

I didn't hear the dressing room door open, but as though on cue

I turned around to see Alana wearing the pantsuit. It fit her perfectly in every way and I knew she liked it. "I'll buy it for you," I said quickly.

"You like it?" she asked.

"Looks great!"

She smiled, then turned and looked at herself in the mirror before returning to the dressing room.

When we had purchased the pantsuit, we went into the feed barn to find Swede. The pain in my abdomen increased and I quickly lost track of the conversation as I tried to maintain my composure and not double up on the floor. Alana called me over to a far corner of the room where Swede stored a magnificent collection of crystal clusters.

"This is the crystal for you," she said, and pointed to a large, milk-white cluster about the size of a dinner plate.

I hesitated, unable to cope because of the pain in my abdomen, but still I tried not to show it.

After a moment she turned away from the crystals, said goodbye to Swede, and went outside. I went with her.

"I'm in terrible pain," I said in a quiet voice, knowing that I had to let her know what was troubling me. I didn't want her to believe that I was sulking about what she had said to me.

She glanced at me. "Where?"

"In my gut," I answered.

We walked on to the Jeep and climbed inside.

"Do you know why it hurts?" she asked.

"No."

"You don't?"

"I guess I could trace it back," I said and leaned forward over the steering wheel. I wasn't sure I could drive until the pain subsided.

"Okay," she said, "you trace it back."

I didn't have far to go. The idea of being a dead student was crushing to me and the more I tried to supress my feelings about it, the greater the pain. I began to cry again as I told her about it, and how more than anything I was totally devoted to my spiritual life, that I had to succeed in it.

"Why are you a dead student?" she asked.

"I don't know, Alana."

"I think you do."

I turned my head to look at her and suddenly recalled the earlier change in the weather that Alana said was a warning.

"If you want to be a good teacher," she said, "you must first be a good student."

I told her that I didn't care whether I was a teacher or not.

"You have to care," she said. "It is your destiny."

I didn't know what to say so I remained silent.

"You resent teachers. Why?"

I lifted my eyes to meet hers and then lowered them again. The pain in my abdomen was unbearable and I began to sob.

Alana waited patiently.

Memories of my childhood confronted me. In particular I saw myself as a young girl attending a Catholic school. My teacher was Mother Superior and she believed that she had a special mission to retrain all left-handed children to be right-handed. Whenever she would see us picking up a pencil with our left hands, she would charge down the aisle with a yardstick and whack the backs of our knuckles. Gradually, all the left-handed students gave in to her except me. The more she struck my left hand bearing the pencil, the tighter I gripped it. As punishment she made me kneel in front of the class all day, every day. The floor became my desk. I was not allowed to sit unless I leaned back on my heels, and very often I wasn't allowed to do that. If I had to be excused to go to the restroom, I had to walk out of the classroom on my knees. On one occasion she forbade me to go to the restroom, telling me that I was only pretending to have to go. After kneeling for a long time with an overfilled bladder, I lost control and had an accident on the floor. From then on her ridicule became brutal and all the other children joined in. Mother Superior explained to the class that I was possessed by a demon and that in order for me to be saved, no one could play with me. She proved her point when she demanded I write a sentence on the blackboard and I wrote the words down backwards. It was, she said, the work of the devil. My "devil words" were a symptom of what is known today as dyslexia. Then, however, it was written in my record that I was a difficult student. As a result, most of the teachers I had after Mother Superior met me with the preconceived notion that I was a trouble-maker. Teachers were my enemies, and I gradually developed attitudes to protect myself from persons in authority.

When I had finished telling Alana my story, the pain in my abdomen had diminished and I got ready to drive out of the parking lot.

"Feel better?" she asked.

I nodded, feeling as though I had touched upon the essence of why and how I had become the person I was today. I began to understand why I had feared Alana, had mistrusted her, and had argued constantly with her.

She changed the subject. "Tell me about your lecture at the university. What is the subject of your speech?"

I hesitated, still thinking about the attitudes I carried from childhood.

"Now that you recognize why you are as you are, let it go," she said.

I nodded obediently, then told her that I had titled my talk

"Between the Wind." But I really didn't think I understood how to function between the wind and so while I was disappointed, I would have to save the subject for another time.

She turned sideways in her seat. Although I knew she was looking directly at me, I kept my eyes on the road. Suddenly I felt better, as though my confession to her freed me from the struggle with the title of my book, freed me from worry or thought, as if a bright, white light had been turned on in my mind, illuminating me so completely that there were no shadows, no attitudes, no opinions to consider. In an abstract way, I realized that the quiet illumination I was experiencing was the state I had been seeking, that I was functioning from consciousness rather than thought, that "between the wind" referred to the flexibility of functioning from this consciousness, and that it meant living between, not within energies outside of my own. I knew in that moment, I was becoming a woman between the wind.

I pulled the Jeep over to the side of the road to turn and gaze at Alana. She pulled her beautiful new pantsuit out of the bag and looked from it to me. "You know why I got this, don't you?" she asked.

"It looks wonderful on you," I said, not really caring what her answer would be. If she wanted to wear it to work with the horses it would be fine with me.

"I thought it would be fun to attend your lecture at the university," she said lightly.

I was surprised, but didn't object.

"You will give a wonderful talk, Heather," she said. "Your realizations will make it so."

"I hope that's true," I answered, "I hope it doesn't wear off. Some realizations have a way of fading."

"And some last a lifetime," Alana added.

"And today's could be a realization of a lifetime."

Alana smiled but did not comment.

"Now that our book is nearly finished, I guess we'll have to think about living a sequel," I said, turning the Jeep back onto the road. A moment later I took a sharp turn to the right. The ranch came into view and, for a moment, I was overcome by the beauty and grandeur of the place.

I stopped at the side of the house. Spirit ran the length of the corral to greet us. Alana opened her door and got out. I watched her, then got out and walked around to the other side of the Jeep and stood next to her.

"Thank you for my horse," I said, watching as Spirit stretched his long neck over the fence in an effort to coax us closer.

Alana went over to the colt and stroked his face. I followed. A hawk soared overhead, casting a shadow on the ground inside Spirit's pen. Alana turned to look at me. "You have a mission, Heather," she said.

I looked at her but didn't speak.

"It will be your task to talk to the people, to share what you have learned," she said. "Your books are only a part of your voice. You must go among the people and speak to them."

I didn't know what to say. I knew that I would do as she asked. She was my teacher, my guide, and my friend. I trusted her and I was filled with gratitude toward her.

"I have something for you," she said and, reaching under the bib of her coveralls, she pulled out a light turquoise T-shirt and held it up in front of me. In the center of the shirt was a large black circle. "I designed the shirt for you," she said, "to remind you of your hole."

I felt a sudden twinge of school-day ridicule and looked away.

"What's the matter?" Alana asked, still holding the shirt in front of me.

The shirt reminded me of how the nuns in school used to mock me and I managed to tell her how I felt about it.

"You don't understand what a hole really is, do you?" she asked.

"I guess not," I answered.

"Then let me tell you again." She paused, gazing deeply at me. "A hole is both negative and positive. A large hole such as this one signifies the root of an individual's life, a person's weaknesses yes, but it also tells the story of a person's strengths. A black hole is a light-catcher. If instead of black the hole was white, you would be wearing a shadow-catcher." She paused again, then added, "I made you a shirt to remind you of your hole and that to fill it, you need only expose it to light."

I gazed into her eyes for a long while, then a light wind picked up a sleeve of the shirt just as I reached for it. "I will wear the shirt as a reminder to try to stay between the wind," I said, wanting to accept her reason for the gift. I didn't want to be offended or suspicious anymore. "I'll wear it as a light-catcher."

Alana smiled, put her arm about my shoulder, and turned me around to look at the colt who was still hanging his head over the fence in an effort to gain attention. "Would you like a lesson with Spirit?" she asked.

"A black hole is a lightcatcher.
...I made you a shirt to remind you
of your hole and that to fill it, you
need only expose it to light."

Please send me the following by HEATHER HUGHES-CALERO:

Quantity	Book Title or Item	Price	Amt.
_____	THE FLIGHT OF WINGED WOLF	9.95	_____
_____	WOMAN BETWEEN THE WIND	9.95	_____
_____	WRITING AS A TOOL FOR SELF-DISCOVERY	9.95	_____
_____	THE GOLDEN DREAM (cloth)	12.95	_____
_____	THE SEDONA TRILOGY:		
_____	Book 1: THROUGH THE CRYSTAL	8.95	_____
_____	Book 2: DOORWAYS BETWEEN THE WORLDS	8.95	_____
_____	Book 3: LAND OF NOME	8.95	_____
_____	DEMYSTIFYING SHAMANISM cassette tape	9.95	_____
_____	DISCOVER YOUR POWER NAME cassette tapes	14.95	_____
_____	COMPANION ENERGY cassette tapes	14.95	_____
_____	SHAMANISTIC TECHNIQUES OF LUCID DREAMING cassette tapes	14.95	_____
_____	WALKING THE PATH OF A SHAMAN cassette tape	9.95	_____
_____	THE STONE GAME pouch	8.95	_____
	SHIPPING: $2.00 one item, $1.00 each additional item.		_____

Check or Money Order. Credit card $25.00 minimum.

TOTAL (USA funds only) $ _____

PHONE ORDERS: 800-336-6015

Please print:

NAME: _____ PHONE:(_____)

ADDRESS: _____

CITY, STATE, ZIP: _____

VISA/MASTERCARD NUMBER: _____

EXP DATE: _____ SIGNATURE: _____

ALSO AVAILABLE AT YOUR BOOKSTORE

Higher Consciousness Books & Seminars
P. O. Box 1797 • Cottonwood, AZ 86326 • 602-634-7728